MY ITALIAN KITCHEN

MY ITALIAN KITCHEN

FAVORITE FAMILY RECIPES

LUCA MANFÉ

Edited by Leda Scheintaub

Photography by Tina Rupp

Stewart, Tabori & Chang | New York

Published in 2014 by Stewart, Tabori & Chang
An imprint of ABRAMS

MasterChef is a trademark of Shine Television, LLC and used under license.
The MasterChef logo is a trademark of Shine Limited and used under license.
All rights reserved. MasterChef is based on a format created by Franc Roddam
in association with Ziji Productions.

© 2014 Shine Television, LLC
All photographs copyright © 2014 Tina Rupp except pages 8, 10, 25, 35, 42,
81, 107, 120, 149, 159, 188, 190, 195, 208, courtesy of Fox

Library of Congress Control Number: 2013952213

ISBN: 978-1-61769-103-4

Editor: Holly Dolce
Designer: Danielle Young
Production Manager: True Sims

The text of this book was composed in FS Clerkenwell, Gotham, and Rollerscript.
Business names, Internet addresses, and telephone numbers given in this book were
accurate at the time it went to press.

Printed and bound in U.S.A.

10 9 8 7 6 5 4 3 2 1

Stewart, Tabori & Chang books are available at special discounts when
purchased in quantity for premiums and promotions as well as fundraising or
educational use. Special editions can also be created to specification. For details,
contact specialsales@abramsbooks.com or the address below.

ABRAMS
THE ART OF BOOKS SINCE 1949
115 West 18th Street
New York, NY 10011
www.abramsbooks.com

To Nonna Anita, thank you for all the good
food and great stories.

To my parents, Bruna and Ferruccio, and to
my sister, Milena, your love and support have
always pushed me to do better.

And to my wife, Cate, because without you,
none of this would have been possible.

CONTENTS

FOREWORD

By Gordon Ramsay

As a small child growing up in Scotland, I remember often being told the Robert the Bruce line "If at first you don't succeed, try, try, and try again." Maybe that saying also made its way over to northeast Italy. It could easily be the mantra of the author of this wonderful cookbook, Luca Manfé.

Luca first tried out for my FOX show, *MasterChef*, in 2012. He made it to the top 100. But I felt he wasn't quite ready to take on the full range of daunting challenges that come with earning a white apron and a place in the *MasterChef* kitchen. So Luca went back to his job managing the front of house at a restaurant in New York City. As he left us on that disappointing day, he told me and my fellow judges, Graham Elliot and Joe Bastianich, that he'd return, stronger and better.

Luca was true to his word. He came back a year later, having spent the intervening time perfecting his craft as a home cook. He wowed us with a highly unusual dish of broccoli rabe ravioli with a pecorino cheese sauce. The pasta was simply perfect. The filling was unusually bright green and had amazing flavor. The sauce was tasty, if a little salty—even for me. But overall, the dish showed great finesse, solid technique, and phenomenal potential. But it wasn't just the dish that I was excited about. I was equally impressed that Luca had swallowed his Italian pride, dusted himself off after his first attempt, and demonstrated the tenacity to come back a year later and give it his all.

Luca went on to crush his competition in more than forty of the most grueling challenges we've ever set on *MasterChef* USA. He had a few wobbles along the way—don't mention the risotto!—but again, his sheer drive and will to succeed, coupled with his unparalleled love of great food, won out. By the time we reached the finale, his confidence had grown, and he had truly mastered his kitchen demons.

In addition to being a great cook and despite English being his second language, Luca has the great gift of charm and communication. His warm personality, stunning dishes, and infectious love of food earned him a legion of fans over the course of the show airing on TV . . . and they, like us, loved watching someone pursue the American dream.

Luca comes from a long line of great Italian home cooks, and many of his inspiring family recipes are featured here in this fantastic book. I hope, like me, you will enjoy this, Luca's first book of recipes, and have successful results when you try them out at home for yourself, your family, and your friends.

FOREWORD

By Joe Bastianich

Italian cuisine is by far the world's most popular food. Beloved and revered everywhere from Macau to South Dakota to London, there is something universally appealing about the delights found within the bounty of the Italian table. It sets the standard for palates everywhere; few other places on earth can lay claim to such treasures as perfectly ripe San Marzano tomatoes from Campania, bright green peppery olive oils from Tuscany, and the decadent aromatic potency of Piedmont's white truffles. Historically the world's food darling, Italy and its exports are showing no signs of relinquishing this heady title.

I've spent my life steeped in all things *cibo Italiano*. It's how I've made my living, my bread and butter, the thing I lay awake thinking about every night. After twenty-odd restaurants (all but two are Italian) the opportunity to be a part of bringing Eataly to New York back in 2010 was one my partners and I didn't hesitate on. We knew full well the intense global appetite for Italian cuisine and products was thriving, as was the common-sense concept of Italian sensibility, and Eataly was clearly the next big thing. Three and half years later, with our Chicago store now open, and expansion plans for Los Angeles, São Paolo, and Philadelphia forthcoming, the proof is really in the pudding. Business for all things Italian is a-boomin'.

That being said, it's only fitting that we find ourselves with our own Italian émigré, Luca Manfé, as America's current MasterChef. Luca hails from Friuli-Venezia Giulia in the northeast corner of Italy, the same region my family is from. A place with a somewhat turbulent past and borders that have changed hands many times in the last century, Friuli is home to a strong and resourceful people who have honed a rich yet often overlooked food culture. When we Americans think of signature Italian dishes, it is usually veal Milanese, Neapolitan pizza, and cacio e pepe from Rome that come to mind. Luca was able to distinguish himself by incorporating regional ingredients to showcase the best of Friuli's specialties and to help introduce dishes such as *frico* and products like prosciutto San Daniele and Montasio cheese to the American public.

Yet Luca, much like his homeland's cuisine, often went unnoticed and underestimated by his competitors.

The culinary world is a cutthroat one, and the *MasterChef* kitchen was no exception. In my four decades in the restaurant business I've pretty much witnessed it all. I've seen every possible underhanded way in which people can scrape themselves forward, and more often than not it's the person who is unafraid to push past moral boundaries who ends up making it in this jungle of an industry. There is a fine line between being a competitor and being a conniver, and it is one that Luca rode well, all while maintaining his integrity. Always taking the high road, Luca persevered by exercising tenacity, focus, and drive, not manipulation. Lighthearted and honest—almost to a fault—Luca was a jubilant presence on set, and after some initial trial and error, it was that jubilance and honesty that came through more and more on the plate. It isn't often we see the honorable emerge victorious, but Luca is proof that nice guys don't always finish last. His skills, rooted strongly in the concept of Italian sensibility, grew immensely during his time on *MasterChef*. Watching him push past his own comfort zone and execute with excellence plates completely foreign to him such as sushi and southern barbecue filled me with immense pride for my fellow *paisan*.

After a devastating rejection at the audition round of season three, yet possessing both the nerve and dedication to show up even stronger for season four, Luca serves as an inspiration to anyone struggling to attain their goals. With the opening of his first restaurant in New York City slated for the coming year, his ability to deliver great food will come full circle. He is the pinnacle of what the winner of *MasterChef* can go on to become, and it is with great pride that I introduce *My Italian Kitchen*, the first of what I hope will be many inspiring culinary contributions to come.

INTRODUCTION

Many things have changed in my life in the last few years, some of which no one could have predicted.

None of my family or friends would have thought that I would be married before my thirtieth birthday. Now, at thirty-three, I have been with my wife, Cate, for more than three blissful years, and we are starting a family!

Nor did any of the people close to me think that I was going to make something big of my life, or that I would have come so far with my passion for food. My friends and family all knew how ambitious I was, but on the day I left Italy ten years ago they couldn't have guessed that I would be crowned America's *MasterChef*. And honestly, I couldn't have either.

I had a dream, but I didn't have a vision. I wanted to make it big, but I really didn't know what I was looking for. Early on, I was in a rush. But after I met Cate I found peace with myself, and I realized that God was going to take care of everything. I trusted in him and simply followed his plan. Never in a million years would I have thought that part of God's plan was a cookbook with my name and face on it!

The day I won the title of *MasterChef*, I was excited beyond belief. Besides my wife's heart, I had never won anything in my life, and now I had just been named the best home cook in America. I soon began to take in what the prize money could mean for my family and me, and then, after a week or so, it dawned on me: "Can you imagine that I will be writing a cookbook?" I said to Cate. "How exciting!"

All of this is beyond what I could have ever expected for my life, but I am having a lot of fun with it, and I sincerely hope it is just the beginning.

This book is the story of the first thirty-three years of my life. In *My Italian Kitchen*, I'll be sharing with you my adventures around my biggest passion: food, ranging from the tiramisù I made with my mother when I was eight years old to the famous basil panna cotta I made to help win me the title of MasterChef. Most of my family memories revolve around food, especially family holidays, and everyone knows how important

food and wine are for Italian culture. I will always remember my Nonna Nori's rabbit stew and my great grandmother Nonna Catina's polenta, and most of all the many dishes I enjoyed from Nonna Anita's kitchen, where I was greeted by a pot on the stove and amazing aromas wafting through the house. Oh, she was such a great cook! Nonna Anita was one of the few people who knew that I'd won the *MasterChef* competition before the final episode aired, and she was so proud of me. Sadly, she passed away just a few weeks before I started writing this book, but I was lucky enough to spend the last days of her life with her. And I was also lucky that my mother knew all of Nonna Anita's recipes by heart and was able to help me put them down on the pages of this book. These are the dishes that I ate growing up, the same ones I crave every time I go back to Italy: classic Italian home cooking.

My mother is an amazing cook as well: Every day when I was growing up, she would wake up early and prepare the food for the day. She also had a full-time job, so she wasn't able to spend hours and hours in the kitchen, but great food was never missing from our fridge. Our food was more practical and surely healthier. To this day, I am amazed at my mother's ability to create a fabulous meal in a short amount of time. My mother is still the first person I call to get advice on what I'm cooking, and the best thing about going back to Italy is when Mom asks me what I would like to eat for dinner. When I cook in my home in New York City, the flavors and smells of my food continue to take me back to her kitchen.

In addition to my family recipes, in this book I'll also be sharing my love for the fantastic region of Friuli-Venezia Giulia and its distinct style of cooking. People from Friuli are hard workers and honest, simple people; back in the day it was all farms and fields, and our food reflects our traditional lifestyle: rustic, humble, rich, and generous. Friuli offers a wide variety of food because it is uniquely situated on the border with the Adriatic Sea in the south, the Alps and Austria in the north, the former Yugoslavia in the east, and Venice in the west. Some of the dishes in the book, such as Frico, *Cotechino* with Sauerkraut, and Spinach Gnocchi with Smoked Ricotta, can only be found in my region, and as you try them you will understand why they are so special to me. You will also learn how to make pasta, because that is what I do best and it's an important part of my Italian heritage. I will demystify the technique and show you how easy it is to make homemade pasta a part of your culinary repertoire.

When I left home, I no longer had my grandmother and mother cooking for me and teaching me. I didn't always have an easy time of it. I remember my first attempts at *penne alla bolognese* and *spaghetti con cozze*. My food was never horrible or inedible—except for a few episodes that my friends can tell you about—but it didn't come close to what it should really taste like. Then I started working in a number of excellent restaurants in Florida, Australia, and then New York. I was never a cook, though; I was always in the front of the house: first a busboy, then a waiter, and last, a manager. I wasn't cooking with my mother anymore, but I was close to very talented chefs. Whenever possible, I would blast them with questions, pick their brains, and attempt to recreate their dishes at home. That's how my path toward *MasterChef* started; many hours in the kitchen plus a dose of sheer determination ultimately got me that coveted white apron.

When I made it into the *MasterChef* kitchen, I was cooking more than I'd ever cooked in my life: seven days a week with three culinary monsters, the judges of the show, Chef Gordon Ramsay, Chef Graham Elliot, and Joe Bastianich, as well as the talented behind-the-scenes team. I learned so much every single day of the three months I spent there, tackling new techniques and cuisines I'd never encountered growing up in Italy, developing my new skill set while remaining true to my Italian roots. The recipes in this book, from my grandmother's apple cake to the sophisticated short ribs I made for the *MasterChef* finale, are a reflection of this journey, the story of my life so far as narrated by food, family memories, and the adventure of a lifetime, winning the title of MasterChef: my very own version of the American dream. Now, friends, it's time to roll up your sleeves, put on an apron, and get cooking!

Buon appetito, beautiful people!

Yours,

Luca

CROSTINI

**RICOTTA, HONEY, AND PINE
NUT CROSTINI**

18

**BEET, GOAT CHEESE, AND
PISTACHIO CROSTINI**

22

**MUSHROOM AND FONTINA
CROSTINI**

24

**GORGONZOLA, ROASTED
PEPPER, AND BALSAMIC
GLAZE CROSTINI**

27

**SAUSAGE, STRACCHINO, AND
RADICCHIO CROSTINI**

30

**TOMATO, MOZZARELLA, AND
SPICY SALAME BRUSCHETTA**

31

Give me a piece of bread, a slice of prosciutto, and a glass of red wine, and I am the happiest man in the world. And here starts the story of crostini: toasted bread dressed up in as many different ways as you can. Crostini is what we eat in Italy when we stop at the bar to have a glass of wine before lunch, a predinner *aperitivo*, or whenever we feel like having a drink and something to nibble.

A classic crostini is made with a slice of prosciutto or other meat. Italy has a huge tradition of cold cuts, commonly called Italian antipasto here in the States but known as *salumi* in Italy. In Italy, our meats are typically prepared on a small scale by farmers who may have a few pigs to spare, and they are shared with family and friends. I always favor meats made locally using the traditional, classic, home-style methods. You won't find these meats in a typical grocery store in the States, but if you live somewhere near an Italian-American community, I am sure you can find an old-school butcher who still makes *sopressa*, *salame*, or *lardo*, just like in Italy.

When you're at the butcher, ask him to cut the meat into paper-thin slices, then buy a long French baguette. When you get home, turn the oven to 375°F (190°C), cut the bread into ½-inch (12-mm) slices, place them on a baking sheet, and toast for about 8 minutes, until golden and crispy. While they are still warm, lay a slice or two of prosciutto or salame or whatever meat you bought over the bread, and there you have it: the most traditional and classic Italian crostini. Then, if you want to take your crostini to another level, read on and try out the recipes in this chapter. The next time you have a get-together at your place, you will blow your friends away with these crostini!

RICOTTA, HONEY, AND PINE NUT CROSTINI

Ricotta, Miele, e Pinoli Crostini

8 French baguette slices
(4 inches/10 cm wide and
½ inch/12 mm thick)

2 tablespoons pine nuts

5 tablespoons (75 ml) extra-
virgin olive oil, plus more for
drizzling

Salt and freshly ground black
pepper

1 cup (240 g) ricotta cheese,
homemade (opposite page)
or good-quality store-bought

2 tablespoons very finely
chopped fresh chives

About 8 teaspoons (40 ml)
pourable honey

Ten years ago, back in Italy, you'd often find me nibbling on ricotta-and-honey crostini at a favorite wine bar in the city of Porcia, where the little bites could be had for just one euro. They fell out of my routine after I moved to the States, until one evening when we were reunited at the bar of a West Village restaurant as I waited for my table. This is my version, elevated with homemade ricotta and a sprinkling of pine nuts for a little extra crunch.

There's nothing that compares to the freshness of homemade ricotta, and it's surprisingly easy to make yourself—no *MasterChef* training required! Just be sure you get the milk to the right temperature and add the correct amount of acidity, and you'll be good to go. See the opposite page for my simple recipe if you'd like to give it a try. I make my ricotta unsalted so I can season it just before serving; I use a fairly heavy hand with the seasoning for a salty ricotta to contrast with the sweet drizzle of honey that tops this crostini. Have fun experimenting with different varieties of honey—my favorites are dark, smoky chestnut honey, and truffle honey; any local honey is going to be fantastic on your crostini.

Makes 8 crostini

Preheat the oven to 375°F (190°C).

Place the bread slices on a baking sheet. Toast the bread in the oven for about 8 minutes, until golden and crisp. Transfer the bread to a plate and let cool. Leave the oven on.

Place the pine nuts in a small bowl. Add a quick drizzle of olive oil and a small pinch of salt and pepper. Arrange the nuts on the baking sheet you used to toast the bread and toast them in the oven for 5 to 8 minutes, until light golden brown. Watch them carefully, as they can go from golden to burned in a heartbeat.

Place the cheese in a medium bowl, add the olive oil, and season with salt and pepper. Mix with a spoon. (Don't whisk, and don't go too crazy with the mixing; otherwise the fat might start to separate.)

Mound about 2 tablespoons of the cheese mixture on each slice of bread and scatter some nuts on top. Finish with the honey, drizzling about 1 teaspoon over each slice.

Homemade Ricotta

I started making my own ricotta after Stacey, a *MasterChef* contestant from Season 3, made a ravioli dish with homemade ricotta in less than an hour in one challenge. As I watched the show, I thought: *Luca, you'd better start making your own ricotta if you ever want to become a MasterChef!*

Ricotta is traditionally made from the whey that's left over from the production of cheese; for homemade ricotta, I cook milk and cream, add vinegar to curdle it, strain it, and squeeze out excess moisture. The result: a fresh cheese that's soft and snowy white with a rich but mild, slightly sweet flavor—a simple Italian classic.

2 quarts (2L) whole milk

1 cup (240 ml) heavy cream

3 tablespoons white-wine vinegar or lemon juice

Makes about 2 cups (480 g)

Set a large strainer over a deep bowl. Dampen a double layer of cheesecloth with water, squeeze out the water, and line the strainer with the cheesecloth.

In a large saucepan, combine the milk and cream. Attach a candy or deep-fry thermometer to the inside of the pan, and cook over medium heat, stirring occasionally, until the mixture reaches 185°F (85°C). Do not let it boil. Turn off the heat, gently stir in the vinegar or lemon juice, and wait for about 2 minutes, until curds form.

Use a large slotted spoon to scoop the curds from the pan to the strainer. Pour the liquidy part remaining in the pan (this is whey) gently over the solids in the strainer and set aside to strain into the bowl for about 20 minutes, occasionally pouring out the whey that drips into the bowl. The longer you let the ricotta drain, the thicker it will be. Gather the edges of the cheesecloth together and gently squeeze out most of the excess liquid.

Use the ricotta immediately, or store it in an airtight container in the refrigerator for up to 5 days. This recipe makes enough for two batches of Ricotta, Honey, and Pine Nut Crostini (opposite page), or just make one batch of crostini and save what's left of the ricotta for one of my ravioli recipes on pages 96–107.

Beet, Goat Cheese,
and Pistachio Crostini
(page 22)

*Ricotta, Honey,
and Pine Nut Crostini
(page 18)*

BEET, GOAT CHEESE, AND PISTACHIO CROSTINI

Barbabietole, Caprino, e Pistacchi Crostini

8 French baguette slices
(4 inches/10 cm wide and
½ inch/12 mm thick)

¼ cup (30 g) shelled unsalted
pistachios

2 teaspoons extra-virgin olive
oil, plus more for drizzling

Salt and freshly ground black
pepper

1 red beet, scrubbed

¾ teaspoon balsamic vinegar

5 fresh mint leaves, very thinly
sliced

½ cup (4 ounces/115 g)
soft fresh goat cheese

Beets and goat cheese is one of my favorite combinations ever, and because crostini are one of my favorite foods to eat, you'll often find a beet-and-goat-cheese crostini being passed around at dinner parties in my apartment in Astoria, Queens. I also like this crostini because it features the colors of the Italian flag!

Caprino, or goat cheese, is made from whole or skim goat's milk. It takes its name from the Italian word for goat, *capra.* For this recipe, I like to use a fresh caprino that's aged for just three or four days and has a soft, creamy texture, but an aged goat cheese that is still spreadable would also be a good choice. Between the creaminess of the cheese, the sweetness of the beets, and the saltiness and crunch of the pistachios, this little bite covers multiple flavor and texture bases. If this recipe gets you craving more of this very Italian combination, see page 80 for my Beet and Goat Cheese Risotto.

Makes 8 crostini

Preheat the oven to 375°F (190°C).

Place the bread slices on a baking sheet. Toast the bread in the oven for about 8 minutes, until golden and crisp. Transfer the bread to a plate and let cool. Leave the oven on.

Place the nuts in a small bowl. Toss them with a quick drizzle of oil and a small pinch of salt and pepper. Arrange the nuts on the baking sheet you used for the bread and toast them in the oven for 8 to 10 minutes, until lightly browned. Remove from the oven and transfer to a small plate to cool. Raise the oven temperature to 450°F (230°C). Roughly chop the cooled nuts.

Wrap the beet in foil, place it on a baking sheet, and roast for about 45 minutes, until cooked through. To check if it is ready, insert a skewer; if it goes in without resistance, the beet is done. Let cool, then remove the beet from the foil and peel off the skin, using your fingers. Cut into ¼-inch (6-mm) cubes and place them in a bowl. Add the oil and vinegar and season with salt and pepper. Stir in the nuts and mint. (You can prepare the beets a day ahead, adding the nuts and mint just before serving.)

Spread 1 tablespoon of the cheese on each slice of bread and top each with some of the beets.

LUCA'S TIPS: When you're peeling the beet, you might want to put on disposable gloves, as beets can color your hands red.

If you are also making the Gorgonzola, Roasted Pepper, and Balsamic Glaze Crostini (page 27), you can make good use of your oven by roasting the peppers for that recipe at the same time.

MUSHROOM AND FONTINA CROSTINI

Funghi e Fontina Crostini

8 French baguette slices
(4 inches/10 cm wide and
½ inch/12 mm thick)

1 tablespoon extra-virgin olive
oil, plus more for brushing

5 ounces (140 g) small
mushrooms, cleaned, trimmed,
and sliced ½ inch (12 mm) thick
(see Sidebar, opposite page)

Salt and freshly ground black
pepper

2 sprigs fresh thyme

2 tablespoons chopped fresh
parsley

2 garlic cloves, halved

8 (⅛-inch-/3-mm-thick) slices
aged fontina cheese (about
1½ ounces/40 g total)

I got the idea for these crostini from Chef Max Convertini of Zio Ristorante in the Flatiron District of Manhattan; he's someone I've gone to again and again over the years for cooking advice. And more than that, he is a very close and generous friend; when I got married, as a gift to my wife, Cate, and me, he cooked an amazing meal for the 130 people at the reception.

You can use any type of mushroom you like for these crostini; I pan sear the mushrooms in a garlic-flavored olive oil for pumped-up flavor and top them with fontina, an Italian cow's-milk cheese made in the Valle d'Aosta region in northwest Italy. Aged fontina, which has a firmer texture than young fontina, is what I recommend.

Makes 8 crostini

Preheat the oven to 375°F (190°C).

Place the bread slices on a baking sheet. Toast the bread in the oven for about 5 minutes, until just golden and crisp. Transfer the bread to a plate and let cool. Raise the oven temperature to 450°F (230°C).

Heat the oil in a large sauté pan over medium-high heat until screaming hot. Add the mushrooms in a single layer, season with salt and pepper, and cook, without moving the mushrooms, for 3 minutes. Stir in the thyme, and cook for 3 to 5 minutes more, stirring often, until the mushrooms are well browned. Remove from the heat and stir in the parsley.

Rub the cut sides of the garlic cloves over the bread slices, then brush the bread with oil and return them to the baking pan. Divide the mushrooms among the bread slices and top each with a slice of the cheese. Bake for 3 to 5 minutes, until the cheese has melted.

LUCA'S TIP: Adding the salt to the mushrooms when they first hit the pan acts to draw their liquid out, leaving them moist inside while they crisp up on the outside.

Should You Wash Mushrooms?

While debated in restaurant kitchens, I remain in the "do not wash mushrooms" camp (with the exception of morels, which need a good soaking in several rinses of water). Mushrooms are like little sponges: If you wash them, they'll absorb the water and refuse to crisp up in the pan. To properly clean mushrooms, you just need a damp paper towel to rub away any dirt, a paring knife to get at any pesky encrusted bits, and a tiny bit of extra patience.

CHECKING IN WITH THE BOSS

There is nothing more exhilarating — or intimidating — than Chef Gordon Ramsay talking to you while you are trying to focus and put a dish together!

GORGONZOLA, ROASTED PEPPER, AND BALSAMIC GLAZE CROSTINI

Gorgonzola, Peperoni Arrosto, e Balsamico

For this recipe, you can buy a jar of marinated roasted bell peppers, but I think it's way cooler if you roast them yourself, and here I'm going to teach you how. I'll also show you how to make your own balsamic glaze; these two techniques will up your Italian cooking skills with little effort!

Gorgonzola is an Italian blue cheese made from whole cow's milk; its flavor is pungent and assertive, and its aroma is strong. It takes its name from the city of Gorgonzola, near Milan, where it was first produced. There are two different kinds of Gorgonzola: *Gorgonzola dolce* (sweet Gorgonzola) and *Gorgonzola piccante*, which is drier and aged longer than dolce. Since it's an intensely flavored cheese, I leave it up to you and your guests to decide how much to spread on your bread. (The original recipe, from a bar where I used to work back in Italy, used mozzarella, but I thought it was way too heavy.) Use less for milder tastes, more for those who like bold flavors; those flavors will get even bolder when drizzled with the deep, dark, slightly sweet balsamic glaze. A glass of red wine is the perfect companion to this crostini.

Makes 8 crostini

Preheat the oven to 450°F (230°C).

Place the bell peppers on the baking sheet and roast for about 45 minutes, turning them with tongs every 15 minutes. The skins will be burned, but don't worry; that's how we want them. Place the peppers in a bowl, cover with plastic wrap, and let cool.

When cool enough to handle and working with one pepper at a time, peel and discard the blackened skin using your fingers or a paper towel. It will take some time, but you'll be happy with the end result. Remove the seeds and membranes. Cut the peppers into ½-inch (12-mm) slices and place them in a medium bowl.

Add the oil, 4 of the smashed garlic cloves, and the basil and season with salt and black pepper. It may look like you're using a lot of oil, but it's OK—this is not a dressing but a marinade. Cover and marinate the peppers in the refrigerator for at least 4 hours or, better, overnight.

(continued)

2 yellow bell peppers

2 red bell peppers

¼ cup (60 ml) extra-virgin olive oil, plus more for brushing

6 garlic cloves, peeled

10 fresh basil leaves, very thinly sliced

Salt and freshly ground black pepper

8 French baguette slices (4 inches/10 cm wide and ½ inch/12 mm thick)

⅓ to ½ cup (2 to 3 ounces/60 to 85 g) Gorgonzola

About 8 teaspoons (40 ml) Balsamic Glaze (page 28)

When you are ready to make the crostini, preheat the oven to 375°F (190°C).

Place the bread slices on a baking sheet and toast the bread in the oven for about 8 minutes, until golden and crisp. Transfer the bread to a plate and let cool. Cut the remaining 2 garlic cloves in half. Rub the cut sides of the garlic on the bread slices, and brush the bread with oil.

Spread the cheese on the bread slices. Arrange the bell pepper mixture over the cheese, alternating colors to up your presentation. Drizzle each with about 1 teaspoon of the balsamic glaze.

Balsamic Glaze
Glassa al Balsamico

2 cups (480 ml) balsamic vinegar

1½ teaspoons honey, plus more as needed

1 bay leaf

Save some of this flavorful glaze for the Prosciutto-Wrapped Figs with Goat Cheese on page 53. You can also drizzle some on grilled steak—one of my favorite ways to use it—or on salad leaves to bring some excitement to an otherwise everyday bowl of greens.

Makes about ½ cup (120 ml)

In a heavy-bottomed medium saucepan, combine the vinegar, honey, and bay leaf. Place over medium heat, bring the mixture to a simmer, and simmer for about 20 minutes, until the vinegar starts to get syrupy and has reduced to about ½ cup (120 ml). Watch carefully near the end, keeping in mind that it will thicken some more as it cools. (If it reduces too much, it will become sticky and harden, and you'll have to start over.) Taste and add some more honey if you feel it is too acidic. Use immediately or store in an airtight container in the refrigerator for up to 6 months. Bring to room temperature before using.

SAUSAGE, STRACCHINO, AND RADICCHIO CROSTINI

Salsiccia, Stracchino, e Radicchio Crostini

8 French baguette slices
(4 inches/10 cm wide and
½ inch/12 mm thick)

8 ounces (225 g) ground pork

2 tablespoons chopped fresh
parsley

¼ teaspoon salt

¼ teaspoon garlic powder

¼ teaspoon onion powder

¼ teaspoon paprika

¼ teaspoon mustard powder

Pinch of ground red pepper

1 teaspoon extra-virgin
olive oil

½ cup (30 g) chopped radicchio

6 ounces (170 g) Stracchino
or other mild creamy Italian
cheese, at room temperature

Crostini are something to nibble on while you have a glass of wine and talk to friends—no big technical concept. It's simple food, and in my house, sausage, Stracchino cheese, and radicchio were never missing from my mother's kitchen, so it was only natural to make crostini with these three ingredients. I enjoyed a version of it at a wine bar called La Curandera in Porcia, Italy, where the sausage came from the butcher just down the road, everything was homemade, and you were guaranteed a great combination of flavors in every bite. For my crostini, I spice up the ground pork with a variety of seasonings for a flavorful sausage, but you can keep it as simple as salt, pepper, and parsley and it will still have a lot going for it. A shortcut would be to use a good-quality preseasoned loose sausage. Stracchino, a creamy, spreadable cheese with a mild and delicate flavor, is typical of the cheeses in the northern regions of Italy; if you can't find it, you can substitute Robiola, Taleggio, or another creamy cheese.

Makes 8 crostini

Preheat the oven to 375°F (190°C).

Place the bread slices on a baking sheet. Toast the bread in the oven for about 8 minutes, until golden and crisp. Transfer the bread to a plate and let cool.

In a medium bowl, combine the pork, parsley, salt, garlic powder, onion powder, paprika, mustard powder, and red pepper. Mix to incorporate the seasoning throughout the pork.

In a medium sauté pan, heat the oil over medium heat. Add the pork and cook, stirring often, for about 10 minutes, until the pork is no longer pink and is starting to brown in places, and the fat has been released. Remove from the heat and toss in the radicchio; stir to wilt the radicchio.

Spread about 1 tablespoon of the cheese on each slice of bread and divide the pork mixture evenly over each slice, pressing down on the pork so it sticks to the cheese and stays put on the bread.

LUCA'S TIP: Use the seasoned pork mixture to make Italian-spiced hamburgers.

TOMATO, MOZZARELLA, AND SPICY SALAME BRUSCHETTA

La Bruschetta Bomba

I had my first real job over school break one summer when I was sixteen. The owner of a local hangout called Sherlock Pub in my hometown of Aviano, in the Friuli region of Italy, asked me if I wanted to work part-time for him as a waiter. It was here that I found my passion for Belgian-style beers, but the best thing about that place was the food, especially the bruschetta. There were ten of them on the menu, Numero 1 to Numero 9, and then there was the bomb: *La Bruschetta Bomba*, piled with spicy salame, mozzarella, and tomatoes (never tomato sauce, as it would make the bread soggy) and topped with oregano and red pepper flakes. (Even though I consider this a crostini, I call it bruschetta because that's what Sherlock Pub called it.) Here is my version of the bomb: flavorful at first bite with the gooey mozzarella stretching out from the bread to your teeth, then after a few seconds—boom!—get ready for the heat!

8 French baguette slices (4 inches/10 cm wide and ½ inch/12 mm thick)

2 garlic cloves, halved

Extra-virgin olive oil

1 ripe tomato, cut into 8 (¼-inch-/6-mm-thick) slices

Red pepper flakes

Fresh oregano leaves

Salt and freshly ground black pepper

16 slices spicy salame or spicy sopressa, cut into ¼-inch- (6-mm-) thick slices

8 (¼-inch-/6-mm-thick) slices fresh mozzarella (about 3 ounces/90 g total)

Makes 8 crostini

Preheat the oven to 375°F (190°C).

Place the bread slices on a baking sheet. Toast the bread in the oven for about 5 minutes, until just golden and crisp. Transfer the bread to a plate and let cool. Leave the oven on.

Rub the bread slices with the cut side of the garlic cloves (the more garlic, the better!), brush the bread with oil, and return the slices to the baking sheet.

Place a tomato slice on top of each slice of bread. You may have to trim them or cut them in half to fit them to the bread. Season with red pepper flakes, oregano, salt, and black pepper. Top each with 2 pieces of the salame or sopressa; as with the tomatoes, you may have to cut the slices to fit atop the bread. Finish each with a slice of the mozzarella— you want the mozzarella slices big enough to almost wrap around the tomatoes and salame.

Bake for about 8 minutes, until the mozzarella starts to melt and brown. If you like, you can finish it off for a minute or two in the broiler to give the cheese topping a nice color. Sprinkle with additional red pepper flakes and oregano and let cool slightly; serve while still warm.

TRAMEZZINI

The first time I took my wife, Cate, to Venice, I made a point to try to stop in every single wine bar we passed along the way. The wine bars of Venice are famous for *cicchetti*, crostini, and tramezzini. Cate was familiar with cicchetti, the Italian version of tapas, and crostini, but she had never seen or heard of tramezzini before. I still remember the day we walked into that first wine bar, its window counter three shelves high with tramezzini showcasing at least twenty different fillings. Cate's face lit up like a kid on her first trip to Disney World.

Tramezzini are the Italian version of English high tea sandwiches. The tramezzino was invented in 1925 in a bar called Caffè Mulassano in Turin and given its name from the famous poet, writer, and politician Gabriele D'Annunzio. *Tramezzino* means "in between," and stands for the food between the bread, but to me it also represents something served in between meals, a little snack. It's one of my favorite bar foods.

For our tramezzini, we use soft white bread without the crust. I find it very hard to find crustless white bread in the States, so I just use regular white sandwich bread and remove the crust. And there is always mayonnaise involved for flavor and to keep the bread moist (I will teach you how to make a healthy mayo to upgrade your tramezzini). My tramezzini, using simple ingredients such as eggs, turkey, cheese, and cured meats (and my favorite, based on shrimp, for something really special) are great snack food for any get-together—easy to put together yet reliably delicious and a guaranteed crowd-pleaser.

EGG AND CHEESE TRAMEZZINO

Tramezzino Vegetariano

Mayonnaise, homemade
(page 37) or good-quality
store-bought

8 slices soft white bread (about
3½ inches/9 cm square), crusts
removed

4 large iceberg lettuce leaves

4 hard-boiled eggs (see
page 36)

Salt and freshly ground black
pepper

⅔ cup (60 g) very thinly sliced
(lengthwise) cornichons

8 slices Emmental cheese

At some point it's inevitable that you will be serving guests who don't eat any type of meat. Besides feeling sorry for them, you should make sure they don't feel left out. I've given you a few vegetarian crostini options, and here is a *tramezzino* that everyone will like. Versions of it can be found in bars throughout Italy.

In Italy, we call Emmental "the cheese with the holes"; it's known for its distinctive flavor and smell and takes its name from the city in Switzerland where it originated. It is a medium-hard cheese that is usually served in thin slices. If unavailable, you could use Leerdammer or even Swiss cheese.

Makes 4 tramezzini

Spread a thin layer of mayonnaise over one side of each bread slice. Add a lettuce leaf (you may have to trim them) on 4 slices of the bread. Pass the eggs through an egg slicer or thinly slice them with a knife and arrange the slices over the lettuce. Season with salt and pepper. Top each with the cornichons and 2 slices of the cheese. Cover with the remaining bread slices, mayonnaise-side down, cut each tramezzino in half, and serve.

VARIATION

Egg Salad Tramezzino: Use the same ingredients, but instead of slicing the egg and pickles, finely chop them and mix them with a tablespoon or two of mayonnaise to make an egg salad filling.

THE *MASTERCHEF* FINALE:

Waiting for the announcement: one of the most nerve-racking and exciting moments of my life!

Elevating an Egg Sandwich

Hard-Boiled and Soft-Boiled Perfection

I love those blogs and websites that tell you how to cook a perfect hard-boiled egg, like you need to be a genius to make one.

If you're going for hard-boiled, place the eggs in a medium saucepan, cover with cold water, and gently bring it to a boil. I like to cook mine for 10 minutes, then take them out of the water, run them under cold water, and crack the shells. Other people will tell you to cook the eggs until the water comes to a boil, turn off the heat, let them sit in the water for a bit, and then shock them in cold water before peeling them. But really, who cares how you cook them? It's a hard-boiled egg! The only important thing is to cook the eggs all the way through following whatever method you like—trust me, it'll be fine.

What takes a little more genius is cooking a perfect soft-boiled egg! In my opinion, there is only one way to cook a perfect soft-boiled egg: Boil and crack a few until you get the right one! It's impossible to give an exact recipe for making a soft-boiled egg because no two eggs are going to be identical, especially if you use free-range farm eggs (and I hope you do!), which vary widely in size, shape, and personality. So bring your pot of water to a boil, gently place the egg in the water, and cook for 5 minutes. Remove the egg from the water with a slotted spoon, run it under cold water, then break the tip with the back of a spoon and dip a small spoon in it. If the yolk is as runny as you like, great. Good job! Otherwise, eat it anyway and try it again with another egg.

Homemade Mayonnaise

Mayonnaise is very easy to make, and it's going to be much easier if your kitchen is outfitted with a food processor or immersion blender with a whisk attachment (my favorite kitchen tool). Otherwise, make sure your arm is well rested, take a hand whisk, and use some good ol' elbow grease. Mayo is nothing more than an emulsion of egg yolk with oil and an acidic element, so make your ingredients matter: Use the freshest farm eggs you can find, and favor organic. Since this mayonnaise won't have any preservatives, it won't last as long as store-bought, so make small batches and make them often, or scale this recipe up if you're making tramezzini for a party.

1 large organic egg yolk

2 teaspoons fresh lemon juice

2 teaspoons apple-cider vinegar

¼ teaspoon Dijon mustard

½ teaspoon salt

1 cup (240 ml) extra-virgin olive oil

Makes about 1 cup (240 ml)

Put the egg yolk in a food processor, or a large bowl if you are whisking with an immersion blender or going low-tech and whisking by hand. Add the lemon juice, vinegar, mustard, and salt. With the food processor running, or while you are whisking, process until the mixture is well blended and bright yellow.

Now we're going to seriously slow things down. Through the food processor's feed tube or while whisking constantly, add ½ cup (120 ml) of the oil *a few drops at a time*; this will take about 4 minutes and a whole lot of patience! Then we get to speed up just a bit—add the remaining ½ cup (120 ml) oil in a very slow, thin stream, processing or whisking all the while, until it is transformed into mayonnaise. Total whisking time will be about 8 minutes if whisking by hand; in the food processor it will be done when all the oil is incorporated. Cover and place in the refrigerator, where it will keep for up to 1 week.

TUNA, CAPER, AND OLIVE TRAMEZZINO

Tonno, Capperi, e Olive Tramezzino

1 (5-ounce/140-g) can tuna in extra-virgin olive oil, drained

1 teaspoon drained and rinsed capers

2 tablespoons thinly sliced (lengthwise) pitted black olives

6 cherry tomatoes, cut into eighths

3 tablespoons very finely chopped red onion

2 teaspoons finely chopped fresh parsley

¼ cup (60 ml) mayonnaise, homemade (page 37) or good-quality store-bought, plus more for spreading

8 slices soft white bread (about 3½ inches/9 cm square), crusts removed

One day I was in a deli in New York and saw a tuna sandwich on the menu. I was confused, thinking seared tuna steak between two slices of bread. Once I understood the concept, I tried it, and it was love at first bite. This is my Italian take on the tuna sandwich that I have become so addicted to since coming to the States. Make sure you use tuna packed in extra-virgin olive oil; the water-packed kind just doesn't make any sense.

Speaking of tuna sandwiches: Have you ever tried the tuna melt with cheddar cheese on a croissant at Dunkin' Donuts? You would not believe how good it is.

Makes 4 tramezzini

Combine the tuna, capers, olives, tomatoes, onions, parsley, and mayonnaise in a medium bowl and mix well.

Spread a light layer of mayonnaise over one side of each slice of bread. Divide the tuna mixture among 4 slices of the bread and top with the remaining bread slices. Cut each tramezzino in half and serve.

VARIATION

Tuna with Pickles Tramezzino: Substitute 1 teaspoon finely chopped pickles for the capers.

SHRIMP IN PINK SAUCE TRAMEZZINO

Gamberetti in Salsa Rosa Tramezzino

Shrimp might not be what pops into your head when you're thinking lunch sandwich. Well, get ready to be surprised—this recipe will open your mind to new sandwich possibilities! Really, just about anything can be put between two slices of bread, and this tramezzino, basically a revisit of the classic shrimp cocktail, is the perfect example. In fact, it is my absolute favorite tramezzino; every time I see it on a bar menu in Italy, I just have to have one or two or three. My recipe, with homemade mayo and fresh shrimp flambéed in brandy, takes this standard bar food up a few notches (with rave reviews from friends at a recent *MasterChef* viewing party), and a little Sriracha adds some kick.

Makes 4 tramezzini

In a medium sauté pan with a lid, heat the oil over medium-high heat until screaming hot. Season the shrimp with salt and pepper and add them to the pan in one layer. Sear on one side for about 2 minutes, until a nice crust has formed (turn one to check). Turn the shrimp and sear for 2 minutes more, until they are just barely cooked through.

Now we'll flame our shrimp for a little excitement and lots of flavor. Turn off the heat and add the brandy. Carefully ignite it with a long kitchen match or a burning wooden skewer. (This is called flambé, and it gives an incredible flavor.) The alcohol should burn off in a few seconds, and the flames will extinguish. If they don't, quickly cover the pan with its lid. When the flames have subsided, turn the heat back to medium-high, add ¼ cup (60 ml) water, and cook for 2 minutes, scraping the pan to remove any browned bits from the bottom. Remove from the heat, drain the shrimp, and let cool.

Cut the shrimp into ¼-inch (6-mm) square bites and place them in a medium bowl. Stir in the mayonnaise, ketchup, Sriracha, and chives.

Divide the shrimp mixture evenly among 4 of the bread slices. Top each with 2 lettuce leaves (you may have to trim them to fit the bread). Spread one side of each remaining slice of bread with a little mayonnaise and use them to top the tramezzini, mayonnaise-side down. Cut each tramezzino in half and serve.

2 tablespoons extra-virgin olive oil

8 ounces (225 g) medium shrimp, peeled and deveined

Salt and freshly ground black pepper

¼ cup (60 ml) brandy

¼ cup (60 ml) mayonnaise, homemade (page 37) or good-quality store-bought, plus more for spreading

1 tablespoon ketchup

1 teaspoon Sriracha®

1 tablespoon finely chopped fresh chives

8 slices soft white bread (about 3½ inches/9 cm square), crusts removed

8 iceberg lettuce leaves

BRESAOLA, ARUGULA, AND GRANA PADANO TRAMEZZINO

Bresaola, Rucola, e Grana Padano Tramezzino

If you don't eat pork, you miss out on the excitement of enjoying the Italian classics—prosciutto, mortadella, and salame—but don't worry. Let me introduce you to *bresaola*: dry-cured beef. It's lean, full of protein, and very healthful, made from the leg of the animal with the fat removed, seasoned with salt and a dry rub, and dry aged for at least thirty days. Bresaola is typically from an area of Italy called Valtellina, which is three hours north of Milano at the border with Switzerland. Remember that Milka chocolate commercial with all the cows in the middle of those beautiful mountains? That is exactly what Valtellina looks like, and it's famous for its many fancy ski resorts and its food and wine. I know Valtellina very well, as I spent a summer there working as a waiter in a hotel for a well-known chef (while I was dating his daughter—that's probably why he never liked me so much). I would eat bresaola on bread for breakfast every day while I was there. Bresaola is always served cold, cut into very thin slices and topped with arugula and shaved cheese, and, long story short, that's where the idea for this tramezzino comes from.

Mayonnaise, homemade (page 37) or good-quality store-bought

8 slices soft white bread (about 3½ inches/9 cm square), crusts removed

2 cups (40 g) arugula

1 tablespoon extra-virgin olive oil

1½ teaspoons fresh lemon juice

Pinch of salt and freshly ground black pepper

4 ounces (115 g) bresaola slices

½ cup (50 g) shaved Grana Padano

Makes 4 tramezzini

Spread a light layer of mayonnaise over one side of each bread slice.

Place the arugula in a medium bowl. Add the oil, lemon juice, and salt and pepper, and toss to coat.

Divide the slices of bresaola evenly among 4 of the bread slices and arrange the arugula on top. Top with the cheese, then cover with the remaining bread slices, mayonnaise-side down. Cut each tramezzino in half and serve.

TURKEY, GORGONZOLA, AND WALNUT TRAMEZZINO

Tacchino Gorgonzola, e Noci Tramezzino

8 slices soft white bread (about 3½ inches/9 cm square), crusts removed

½ cup (3 ounces/85 g) Gorgonzola, at room temperature .

¼ cup (25 g) walnuts, crushed with the bottom of a glass

4 ounces (115 g) sliced turkey breast

The first time I had a turkey tramezzino was when I took a trip home to Italy with my wife, Cate, who doesn't eat pork but loves turkey. When I got back to the States, I looked at all the different types of turkey meat on display at the deli counter and had some fun experimenting with my turkey tramezzini: Feel free to spice up the recipe however you like, using maple-glazed turkey, cracked black pepper turkey, smoked turkey, Cajun-spiced turkey, or even slices of chicken breast, if you'd like. I pair the turkey with Gorgonzola for added flavor, but if you aren't a fan of this pungent and stinky cheese, goat cheese or any creamy cheese you like could be substituted.

Makes 4 tramezzini

Spread one side of each slice of bread with 1 tablespoon of the cheese. Sprinkle 1 tablespoon of the nuts over 4 of the bread slices. Top the nuts with some of the turkey and cover with the remaining bread slices, cheese-side down. Cut each tramezzino in half and serve.

THE POLKA DOT CHALLENGE

Yasmin, one of the producers of the show, picked this shirt for me to wear. "I am not wearing polka dots," I told her as she handed me the shirt. I guess you can tell who won that battle.

PROSCIUTTO AND MUSHROOM TRAMEZZINO

Prosciutto e Funghi Tramezzino

If you ask ten Italians what their favorite pizza was when they were a kid, at least six of them would answer "*prosciutto e funghi.*" When I was little, it was the only pizza I'd eat, so using these two ingredients—prosciutto and mushrooms—in a tramezzino is really just an extension of the pizza concept. Most of the bars in Italy use mushrooms out of a jar, because they figure their flavor will be disguised by the mayo, anyway, but for my tramezzino, we'll cook up fresh mushrooms and mix them with homemade mayonnaise to turn this standard Italian bar food into something to really be proud of.

Prosciutto cotto is like an Italian ham, but not really, because American ham doesn't taste like anything close to prosciutto cotto! While, to me, most American ham is more like bologna, Italian ham has lots of aromatics used to age it and has way more fat, which makes it much more flavorful.

Makes 4 tramezzini

In a large sauté pan, heat the oil over low heat. Add the garlic, rosemary, and thyme. (We use low heat so the oil can take on the flavors of the herbs fully.) When the garlic has browned a bit, raise the heat to high.

When the pan is screaming hot, add the mushrooms, season with salt and pepper right away so they begin to release their liquid, and cook, without moving them, for 3 minutes, so they form a nice crust. Stir and continue to cook for 5 minutes more, or until the mushrooms are nicely softened and browned all over. Remove from the heat and fish out the garlic, rosemary, and thyme. Transfer the mushrooms to a bowl and let cool. Stir in the mayonnaise.

Spread a light layer of mayonnaise over one side of each bread slice. Divide the mushroom filling among the bread slices, then top each with 4 slices of the prosciutto. Cover with the remaining bread slices, mayonnaise-side down. Cut each tramezzino in half and serve.

2 tablespoons extra-virgin olive oil

4 garlic cloves

2 sprigs fresh rosemary

2 sprigs fresh thyme

1 pound (455 g) cremini or baby portobello mushrooms, cleaned, trimmed, and cut into small cubes (see page 25)

Salt and freshly ground black pepper

2 tablespoons mayonnaise, homemade (page 37) or good-quality store-bought

8 slices soft white bread (about 3½ inches/9 cm square), crusts removed

16 slices (about 4 ounces/ 115 g) prosciutto cotto

ANTIPASTI

ARUGULA, PEAR,
AND GRANA PADANO
SALAD

46

ASPARAGUS
AND GOAT
CHEESE FRITTATA
WITH ARUGULA
SALAD

47

CHEESE-FILLED
ARTICHOKE
BOTTOMS

51

PROSCIUTTO-
WRAPPED FIGS
WITH GOAT
CHEESE

53

MY GRANDMOTHER'S
FRIED EGGPLANT

56

BAKED SCALLOPS
AU GRATIN

58

SWEET-AND-SOUR
SARDINES

60

CLAMS AND MUSSELS
WITH CHERRY
TOMATOES IN WHITE
WINE BROTH

63

FRIED MIXED
SEAFOOD WITH
MARINARA SAUCE

66

The definition of an *antipasto* is something that comes before the pasta, but it is really anything that you would start the meal with. My mother's artichokes filled with cheese and the figs wrapped in prosciutto are a couple of my favorite antipasti, perfect little bites to get you excited about your meal. With my seafood antipasti you will get a taste of the flavors you'd find on a trip along the Adriatic coast from Trieste to Venice, and if you close your eyes when you make the clams and mussels brodetto, you can think you are in a restaurant on the beach with your feet in the sand. My grandmother's fried eggplant and sweet-and-sour sardines takes me back to her kitchen.

The antipasto sets the tone of your meal. When I eat at a restaurant, I try to make my food choices flow from one to the next: If I order a plate of raw fish for an appetizer, I most likely will choose a fish as my main course, but if I start with something heavier and more flavorful, I will certainly pick a meat dish as my *secondo*. I do the same when choosing menus to cook for my friends and when I compose my Dinners with Luca. In this chapter there's something for every season and taste, all full of flavor and designed to lead you in to the next tasty dish as you build a multicourse Italian dinner. Or simply enjoy them on their own!

ARUGULA, PEAR, AND GRANA PADANO SALAD

Insalata di Rucola, Pere e Grana Padano

FOR THE VINAIGRETTE

1½ teaspoons grated lemon zest

2 tablespoons fresh lemon juice

½ teaspoon Dijon mustard

Salt and freshly ground black pepper

¼ cup (60 ml) extra-virgin olive oil

FOR THE SALAD

4 cups (80 g) arugula

1 large Bartlett pear, halved, cored, and very thinly sliced lengthwise

Small hunk of Grana Padano

This is something my mother would serve on a hot summer day. It's a classic pairing of Italian ingredients and a great way to highlight first-of-season pears. It's easy to put together, refreshing, light, and absolutely delicious.

Serves 4

FIRST, WE'LL MAKE THE VINAIGRETTE:
Combine the lemon zest, lemon juice, mustard, salt, and pepper in a small bowl, then slowly add the oil and whisk until it's incorporated.

THEN WE'LL MAKE THE SALAD:
In a large bowl, toss the arugula and pears together; add the vinaigrette and toss to coat.

Arrange the salad on a large oval serving plate with most of the arugula in the center and the pears scattered around the plate. Using a vegetable peeler, generously shave cheese over the top. Serve immediately.

Arugula: A Stand-Up Salad Green

You'll notice that my salad recipes inevitably call for arugula. Well, what do you expect? I'm Italian! But more than that, to me, arugula, with its pungent, peppery flavor, has more personality than any other lettuce or mixed greens. I like a salad that does more than just show up; it should stand up to complement the main dish, and arugula never fails me, no matter what I serve it with.

ASPARAGUS AND GOAT CHEESE FRITTATA WITH ARUGULA SALAD

Frittata con Asparagi e Caprino con Rucola

When I got married, eggs became a much bigger deal in my life, especially for breakfast. Scrambled, sunny-side up, omelets, cheese-and-egg sandwiches; I'm sure you are all very familiar with these American morning favorites. But did you know that in Italy we almost never serve eggs for breakfast? A typical Italian breakfast is cereal with milk or coffee and cookies; when I'm back home in Aviano, Friuli, my favorite is a trip to the local pastry shop, Pasticceria da Stradella, for cappuccino with a chocolate croissant or a German-style cream- or chocolate-filled doughnut called *krapfen*, the kind without the hole in the middle. (At home in Astoria, I get mine at Gianpiero Bakery on 30th Avenue, which, back in the day, was a superfamous New York Italian street.)

Anyway, this recipe is not about breakfast or sweet treats, but rather about showing you how we like to use eggs in Italy. A frittata, an open-faced omelet or quiche without the crust, is one of our favorite ways to serve our eggs (and a frittata, made with tomatoes and potatoes, was what I made for my first *MasterChef* Mystery Box dish). I would not suggest making this recipe for breakfast; instead, serve it with a fresh, leafy salad for a simple and tasty lunch, which will be noticeably tastier if you seek out and use local and organic eggs.

Serves 4 to 6

FIRST, WE'LL MAKE THE FRITTATA:

Fill a large bowl with ice and water to make an ice bath. Bring a large pot of water to a boil. Add the asparagus and cook for about 3 minutes, until slightly softened and bright green in color. Using a slotted spoon, transfer the asparagus to the prepared ice bath. Let cool for a minute, then, using a slotted spoon, remove the asparagus and pat dry with a paper towel. Chop the asparagus.

Beat the eggs in a large bowl. Add the cream, goat cheese, Grana Padano, mustard, Sriracha, thyme, salt, and a nice amount of pepper and whisk to incorporate the ingredients.

(continued)

FOR THE FRITTATA

½ bunch (about 7 ounces/ 200 g) asparagus, woody ends trimmed (see Note, page 48)

10 large eggs

¼ cup (60 ml) heavy cream

½ cup (4 ounces/115 g) soft fresh goat cheese, crumbled

¼ cup (25 g) freshly grated Grana Padano

1 teaspoon Dijon mustard

2 teaspoons Sriracha

1 tablespoon fresh thyme leaves

½ teaspoon salt

Freshly ground black pepper

3 tablespoons unsalted butter

FOR THE SALAD

4 cups (80 g) arugula

1 cup (150 g) cherry tomatoes, halved

½ red onion, very thinly sliced

½ cup (20 g) thinly sliced fresh basil leaves

2 tablespoons extra-virgin olive oil

2 teaspoons balsamic vinegar

Salt and freshly ground black pepper

Melt 2 tablespoons of the butter in a large nonstick pan over medium-high heat, swirling it so the butter coats the entire surface of the pan as well as the sides. Spread the asparagus in an even layer on the bottom of the pan, then pour the egg mixture over the asparagus. Cook for 3 minutes without touching it, then use a spatula to make a few holes in the bottom so any still-raw egg can get to the bottom of the pan. (This must be done up front, not later, because now is when you need to make a nice, even base for your frittata.) Reduce the heat to low, cover the pan, and cook for about 10 minutes, until the bottom is set. Once the bottom is set, it's time to turn over your frittata. Place a large round plate upside down on top of the pan. Turn off the heat, then very rapidly invert the pan and the plate together so the frittata ends up on the plate.

Return the pan to the stove and melt the remaining 1 tablespoon butter, swirling it to coat the bottom of the pan. Slide the frittata back into the pan. Cover and cook until the second side is set, about 5 minutes.

Rinse the serving plate you used to flip the frittata, return the frittata to the plate, and cut the frittata into slices.

THEN, TO MAKE THE SALAD:

In a large bowl, combine the arugula, tomatoes, onions, and basil. In a small bowl, whisk the oil into the vinegar and season with salt and pepper. Toss the dressing into the salad and serve alongside the frittata slices.

VARIATION

You can make the frittata with any number of fillings, and it's a great way to make use of leftover vegetables. I love mine with mushrooms, cooked as I do on page 170; sausage and peppers, or spinach simply sautéed with garlic are also good options.

NOTE: Save the woody asparagus ends for making stock for the Asparagus and Lemon Risotto on page 82.

LUCA'S TIP: For a perfect frittata, you absolutely need a good nonstick pan and a bit of patience while the bottom cooks into a nice, even crust and the egg gently comes together until it is just set.

CHEESE-FILLED ARTICHOKE BOTTOMS

Cuori di Carciofi con Formaggio

The last time I was back in Italy with my wife, Cate, it was artichoke season, and we were lucky enough to be served this dish at my mother's table. Whenever I eat it, I'm reminded of the magical flavors my mother brings to the plate using the simplest of ingredients. Mom uses creamy, pale yellow Montasio cheese, which is typical of Friuli, but you can use any medium-soft, not-too-aged cheese such as Fontina, Fiore Sardo, Asiago, or even Caciotta.

At the produce markets in Italy, vendors will have artichoke bottoms prepped and ready for you to use. I've never seen this here in the States, so I guess you will have to learn how to clean an artichoke! But don't worry; it's not really all that difficult if you follow the directions I've given here. OK, maybe it *is* sort of a pain in the neck, and I know some of you are wondering how the heck you actually eat them, but after a few artichokes, you'll learn fast. Then it becomes another easy recipe you have under your belt with a very tasty reward at the end of your labor.

Makes 4 stuffed artichokes

Preheat the oven to 400°F (205°C).

Fill a large bowl with water and squeeze in the juice from 1 of the lemons. Add the squeezed lemon halves, too. (This makes acidulated water into which we'll toss the artichokes as they are prepped to keep them from oxidizing, or browning.)

Cut away the end of the stem of an artichoke, leaving about 1 inch (2.5 cm). Working from the bottom of the artichoke head and moving around and upward, grasp and break off the tough outer leaves to reveal the soft inner leaves. Grab these inner leaves and remove them, watching out for their sharp tips, to reveal the fuzzy choke (which is inedible; we'll get to that in a minute). Trim away any outer leaves remaining by holding a paring knife at a 45-degree angle and turning the artichoke against the knife. The bottom should now be bare, smooth, and flat. Peel the stem and scoop out the fuzzy choke by inserting the tip of a paring knife just below the surface of the fuzzy layer and making small turns of the artichoke to slice off the choke (alternatively, you can scoop the choke out with a kitchen spoon). You'll see a dimpled layer under the choke; scrape this off until a smooth white surface is revealed. Immediately place the artichoke in the lemon water, then repeat with the remaining artichokes.

(continued)

2 lemons, halved

4 medium artichokes

1 tablespoon whole peppercorns (black, pink, or rainbow)

2 garlic cloves

2 bay leaves

2 tablespoons extra-virgin olive oil

Salt and freshly ground black pepper

½ cup (120 ml) white wine

½ to ¾ cup (5 to 8 ounces/ 140 to 210 g) finely chopped Montasio cheese, or other medium-soft cheese

Shaved Grana Padano

2 tablespoons chopped fresh parsley

Fill a medium saucepan with water and add the remaining 2 lemon halves, the peppercorns, garlic, and bay leaves and bring to a boil over medium-high heat. Add the artichokes, reduce the heat to medium, and simmer for about 5 minutes, until tender. Lift out the artichokes and pat dry with paper towels.

Heat the oil in a large ovenproof sauté pan over medium-high heat. Season the artichokes with salt and pepper and place them stem-side up in the pan. Sear for about 2 minutes, until nicely colored. Flip the artichokes and sear for 2 minutes more, or until nicely colored on the second side. Pour the wine into the pan and turn off the heat.

Fill each artichoke bottom with 2 to 3 tablespoons of the Montasio, depending on the size of the artichoke. Don't worry if it seems like a lot, because the cheese will melt down when you cook it. Sprinkle some Grana Padano on top of each artichoke. Place the pan in the oven and bake for 8 to 10 minutes, until the cheese starts to melt.

Transfer the artichokes to four individual plates and sprinkle evenly with the parsley. Drizzle some of the juices from the pan on top and serve.

VARIATION

Seared Artichokes: After you've cleaned and simmered the artichokes, instead of filling and baking them, simply chop and sear them in some olive oil in a screaming-hot pan until browned all over. Finish with a sprinkle of salt and pepper, fresh basil, a dusting of cheese, and a squeeze of lemon.

PROSCIUTTO-WRAPPED FIGS WITH GOAT CHEESE

Fichi con Prosciutto e Caprino

I'm crazy about figs—there are few things I enjoy more than eating a freshly picked fig. This fig mania comes from my father. When my parents bought a new house in Friuli more than ten years ago, my father completely redid the yard. The only trees he didn't touch were the old cherry tree, the hazelnut tree, and the kiwi tree. As my mother was coming up with a wish list of flowers and plants for the garden, my father wanted just one thing: a fig tree. The first year, his fig tree grew super-fast but produced no fruit. The second year, it grew even more and gave us one fig. My father warned us: "No one is allowed to eat that fig. That's my fig."

Figs are one of the first signs that summer is almost over and we are heading into fall, my most anticipated food season of the year. There are three fig trees on the street on which I live in Astoria, Queens, and I am sorry, neighbors, but I've eaten every one of their figs since I moved in seven years ago.

The first time I ate figs wrapped with prosciutto was at a restaurant in Sydney, Australia, but it's a classic recipe that you can find just about anywhere. The typical Italian version calls for Gorgonzola, but I find milder goat cheese gives a better balance and just the right amount of creaminess. Ask your butcher for very thin slices of prosciutto that are 7 to 8 inches (17 to 20 cm) long; if they are shorter, you may need a couple of slices per fig.

Serves 4

Preheat the oven to 375°F (190°C).

LET'S PREP THE FIGS:

Cut the stems off the figs and cut them down the middle almost but not all the way through. Make an indentation in the middle of each fig half for the goat cheese to fit in nicely. Scoop 1 teaspoon of goat cheese, roll it with your fingers into a ball, and put it in the indentation you made in the fig. Close the fig. Do the same with the remaining figs. Wrap one slice of the prosciutto around each fig. Set aside on a plate.

(continued)

FOR THE FIGS

12 black Mission figs

¼ cup (2 ounces/55 g) soft fresh goat cheese, at room temperature

12 very thin slices prosciutto di San Daniele or prosciutto di Parma

Extra-virgin olive oil for sautéing

FOR THE VINAIGRETTE

2 tablespoons white wine vinegar

½ teaspoon honey

½ teaspoon Dijon mustard

1 small garlic clove, minced

2 drops Tabasco

¼ teaspoon salt

¼ teaspoon freshly ground black pepper

¼ cup (60 ml) extra-virgin olive oil

FOR THE SALAD

4 cups (40 g) mixed greens

2 cups (300 g) cherry tomatoes, halved

TO SERVE

Drizzle of Balsamic Glaze (page 28)

NOW PREPARE THE VINAIGRETTE:

Combine the vinegar, honey, mustard, garlic, Tabasco, salt, and pepper in a small bowl, then whisk in the oil until emulsified.

AND COOK THE FIGS:

Drizzle just a little oil in a large sauté pan and heat it over medium-high heat until screaming hot. Add the figs (you may need to cook them in batches) and cook until crisp on all sides, turning the figs with tongs, about 4 minutes. The fat will render and the prosciutto will get crisp very quickly, so make sure you turn the figs before the prosciutto starts to burn. Transfer the pan to the oven and bake for 2 to 3 minutes, until sizzling hot all over.

WHILE THE FIGS ARE IN THE OVEN, WE'LL GET THE SALAD READY:

In a salad bowl, combine the mixed greens and tomatoes, add enough of the vinaigrette to coat, and toss.

TO SERVE:

Divide the salad among four plates, centering it in the middle, and arrange 3 figs per plate around the salad. Drizzle the figs with a little Balsamic Glaze, and serve.

VARIATION

Prosciutto-Wrapped Figs with Goat Cheese Sauce: Instead of filling the figs with goat cheese, make a sauce out of the goat cheese by melting it in a small saucepan with a little cream to thin it. Pour the sauce over the figs and serve the salad on the side.

MY GRANDMOTHER'S FRIED EGGPLANT

Le Melanzane della Nonna

1 pound (455 g) baby eggplant, Italian eggplant, or light purple eggplant

Salt

1 quart (960 ml) peanut or vegetable oil, for frying

2 large eggs

1 cup (240 ml) whole milk

1 tablespoon grappa (optional)

1⅓ cups (165 g) all-purpose flour

Freshly ground black pepper

This recipe, a very easy tempura-style eggplant that makes the most of the flavor and texture of the vegetable, is a tribute to Nonna Anita. My grandmother would use large globe eggplants for slices as big as steaks; my preference is for baby eggplant or Italian eggplant for a sweeter, less-bitter flavor. Both will be winners if you follow the frying tips I've shared with you below.

Serves 4

Line a baking sheet with paper towels.

Take a vegetable peeler and run it in a circle around the bottom of the eggplant to remove the peel from the base of the eggplant. Leave about ½ inch (12 mm) of skin in place directly above the spot that you just peeled. Then run the peeler around the eggplant again above the unpeeled spot. Repeat, going up the eggplant, leaving you with a striped eggplant. Now take a knife and make ½ inch (12 mm) cuts the length of the eggplant to make half-peeled–half-unpeeled pieces of eggplant. Place the eggplant on the baking sheet and sprinkle with salt, cover with another layer of paper towels, place another baking sheet on top, and place a heavy object like a can of tomatoes on top to weight the eggplant. The salt and the weight will help release the water from the eggplant. Set aside for 2 hours.

Heat the oil in a deep-fryer or in a shallow saucepan over medium-high heat, until a deep-fry thermometer registers 350°C (175°C). Rinse and dry one of the baking sheets and line it with paper towels.

In a shallow bowl, whisk the eggs with the milk and grappa, if using. Add a pinch of salt, then gradually incorporate the flour, whisking the whole time.

Dip the eggplant slices in the batter one at a time, coating them on both sides and then lifting them a few inches above the bowl to drain excess batter. As each is coated, place it in the oil. Be especially careful with the first slice, as the oil may splash a bit.

If you are using a deep-fryer, take the basket out, then drop the eggplant slices directly in the oil, press them down into the oil with a spoon for 10 seconds, and then set the basket on top of them so they'll be completely submerged in the oil. (If you're using a saucepan, just add the eggplant slices directly to the oil.) Turn after 3 to 4 minutes; when they are golden brown all over, remove them from the oil using tongs or a slotted spoon and rest them on the lined baking sheet. Season with salt and pepper when still super-hot and serve immediately.

Taking the Fear out of Frying

Many people are intimidated by frying, but it's really not that hard to do at home. Here are some pointers to help you get the best results: Avoid overheating the oil—when the oil reaches the burning point, it begins releasing free radicals (not good!), so if you see smoke rising from the pot, carefully discard the oil and start all over again. One way to avoid smoking your oil is to make sure you have a light coating of flour on whatever you're frying. Shake off all excess before it goes in to fry, as too much flour can make your oil burn. Equally important is bringing the oil back up to the frying temperature, in this case 350°C (175°C), between batches to keep each new addition just as crisp as the first.

BAKED SCALLOPS AU GRATIN

Cappesante Gratinate

13 medium scallops in the shell

⅓ cup (40 g) fine bread crumbs

3 tablespoons chopped fresh parsley, plus more for serving

3 tablespoons freshly grated Grana Padano, plus more for sprinkling

1 tablespoon finely grated lemon zest

3 tablespoons white wine

2 garlic cloves, halved

¼ cup (60 ml) extra-virgin olive oil

Salt and freshly ground black pepper

You don't often find scallops on the shell in restaurants in the States, so it's an appetizer that I often order when I find myself in a seafood restaurant back home in Italy. This is a quick and easy recipe, but at the same time it's elegant enough to serve to any discerning guest. You will need to buy fresh scallops in the shell for this dish, so call your fish market a few days in advance and ask them to order some for you.

Why thirteen scallops? I always make an extra one for tasting at the moment the timer rings, as scallops are something you want to get exactly right: medium-rare, translucent, meltingly tender. When you have it, stop right there and take them out of the oven. Leave them in any longer and they will be overcooked and rubbery, so be sure to stay close to the kitchen for those important twelve minutes!

Serves 4

Preheat the oven to 400°F (205°C).

Before anything else, we'll prep our scallops. Make sure all the scallops are tightly closed; if any are open, do not use them. Have a bowl of cold water ready, and line a plate with paper towels. With a clean dish towel, pick up a scallop and hold it in one hand. With the other hand, insert a paring knife or oyster knife, if you have the latter, into the front of the scallop shell, scraping along the top of the shell and turning the shell as you move the knife to open it. Carefully remove the top shell and discard it. Use a small spoon to gently scrape the scallop from the shell, setting the bottom shell aside. Gently tear off the membrane skirt from the scallop and place the scallop into the bowl of cold water to wash away any grit. Using your knife, remove the muscle from the side of the scallop. Place the scallop on the paper towel–lined plate and repeat with the remaining scallops. Rinse the reserved bottom shells very well in hot water and pat them dry with paper towels. Place the shells on a baking sheet and return the scallops to the shells.

To make a coating for the scallops, combine the bread crumbs, parsley, cheese, lemon zest, wine, garlic, oil, and salt and pepper in a food processor and process for about 1 minute, until the ingredients are well-incorporated.

Cover the scallops completely with the bread-crumb mixture, dividing it evenly among the shells. Sprinkle some extra cheese on top; it will give the topping a nice au gratin look. Bake for 12 minutes. Take one scallop out of the oven and cut it in half. You're aiming for medium-rare, when the inside of the scallop is translucent. When you're there, immediately remove the scallops from the oven. You may want to move the scallops to the broiler for the last minute to make sure they are nicely browned on top.

Arrange the scallops on four individual plates (be careful when you handle them, as the shells will be very hot), sprinkle some parsley on top, and serve.

Screaming Hot and Quick

When I'm not baking my scallops, I cook them as Chef Gordon Ramsay taught me. If you follow him at all, you know that he loves his scallops. You might remember the *MasterChef* challenge where Natasha had the assignment of making Chef Ramsay's signature seared scallop salad with confit potatoes and black truffles—not an easy one to pull off (but she did an amazing job!). The secret to seared-scallop perfection is to cut the scallops in half, season them, and cook them in a drizzle of olive oil in a screaming hot pan for not even 2 minutes per side, until they are medium-rare and translucent inside, and then serve them as soon as they come out of the pan.

SWEET-AND-SOUR SARDINES

Sarde in Saor

1 quart (960 ml) vegetable or peanut oil, for frying

12 whole fresh sardines, cleaned and deboned

Salt and freshly ground black pepper

All-purpose flour

2 tablespoons extra-virgin olive oil

2 large white onions, thinly sliced

¾ cup (110 g) golden raisins, soaked in water to cover for 30 minutes, then drained

¾ cup (90 g) pine nuts

½ cup (100 g) sugar

2 cups (480 ml) apple-cider vinegar or white-wine vinegar

1 cup (40 g) finely chopped fresh parsley

This is a classic Venetian dish going way back. There are references to it in novels from the 1300s and the eighteenth-century poetry of Carlo Goldoni, and it's still wildly popular in twenty-first-century Venice, where you'll often see sardines arranged in a glass bowl marinating on the counter of a wine bar. The name comes from the Venetian dialect and translates to "sardines in flavors"; a sweet-and-sour sauce is poured on top of fried sardines, and the sardines are left to marinate for several hours. The longer you marinate your sardines, the better they will taste, so be sure to plan your *sarde in saor* in advance.

This dish brings back memories of Nonna Anita, who used to prepare it all the time when I was growing up. She would remove the bones from the sardines with her fingers, fry the sardines, and leave them to marinate for what seemed like forever. Though I was never the biggest sardine fan, I always loved her sarde in saor—part of it must have been the anticipation of waiting for the moment Nonna gave the OK to dig in!

Serves 6

In a deep-fryer or a shallow saucepan over medium-high heat, heat the vegetable or peanut oil until a deep-fry thermometer registers 375°C (190°C). Line a baking sheet with paper towels.

While the oil is heating up, season the sardines with salt and pepper and dust them with flour. Working in batches of four, gently place them in the oil, one at a time. Cook for 5 minutes, turning them once, until crisp. Remove them from the oil using a slotted spoon, lay them on the lined baking sheet, and immediately season them with salt. Season and fry the remaining sardines and set aside on the baking sheet.

In a medium saucepan, bring 2 cups (480 ml) water to a simmer. Adjust the heat as needed to maintain a simmer.

In a large sauté pan, heat the olive oil over medium-high heat. Add the onions, season them with salt (it's best to salt them right away to get their moisture out), and cook until they have begun to caramelize and are just a tiny bit burned in places (don't be afraid of a little char—this adds a lot of flavor!), about 20 minutes. When the pan gets very dry, add enough of the hot water to cover the onions, and stir to release the browned bits from the bottom of the pan. Keep on cooking, adding more water as needed, for about 10 minutes, until the onions are very soft.

Stir in the raisins and nuts, then add the sugar and vinegar and stir constantly until the sugar has dissolved, about 5 minutes, adding more hot water if the mixture starts to stick to the pan. Give it a taste and add some salt, if needed—remember, we are going for a good balance of sweet and sour. Remove from the heat and let cool completely.

Coat a small glass casserole dish with a thin layer of the onion mixture, then add a layer of 4 sardines. Continue layering the remaining onions and sardines, finishing with a layer of onions. Cover and refrigerate for at least 8 hours or overnight. Remove from the refrigerator about 1 hour before serving to bring the sardines to room temperature; sprinkle with the parsley just before serving.

VARIATION

The sardines are great served on toasted baguette slices as crostini. If you visit Venice's wine bars, you will find them everywhere!

LUCA'S TIP: If possible, ask your fish market to clean and debone the sardines for you. If not, it is very easy for any home cook to do: Cut the sardines in half lengthwise, rinse them well, and, using a small knife, cut around the spine and pull it out with your fingers, and open up the sardines like a book.

CLAMS AND MUSSELS WITH CHERRY TOMATOES IN WHITE WINE BROTH

Cozze e Vongole al Vino Bianco

This is one of my favorite seafood appetizers, one we'll always order back home on the Adriatic coast after a long day at the beach. The recipe gives instructions for plating into individual serving bowls, but it also could be served in one big bowl, family-style, for everyone to hungrily dig into.

I confess, my favorite thing about the dish is the bread. I hurry to eat all the seafood so I can get to the broth-soaked crostini at the bottom of the bowl, and when that's devoured, I start dipping in more and more bread until all the broth is gone. When I'm finished, I feel like I've eaten three bowls of pasta and am about to blow up! (If I want to lighten things up, I'll just drink the rest of the broth from the bowl.) At home, be sure the mussels and clams are completely cleaned of sand; a mouthful of sand as you slurp up the juices can turn one of the best possible appetizers into one of the worst!

Bring out the largest pot you have for making this dish, as you'll need plenty of room for the mussel and clam shells to open as they cook. For the wine, I like a nice pinot grigio, chardonnay, or Tocai Friulano from my native Friuli region—finish the bottle at the table or sip it stove-side to get the party rolling before you've left the kitchen.

Serves 8

Slice the bread on the diagonal into 4-inch-wide (10-cm) by ½-inch-thick (12-mm) slices. You will need at least 48 slices of bread (4 per serving), and you'll have plenty of extra for sopping up the juices.

In a large sauté pan, heat 1 tablespoon of oil over medium-high heat. Arrange 8 slices of bread in the pan and toast them for about 4 minutes, until golden brown and crisp. Sprinkle another tablespoon of oil over top of the bread slices, then flip them and toast until golden brown and crisp on the second side, about 4 minutes more. The idea is to soak the bread in olive oil, then crisp it up on the outside so the bread is crunchy outside and nice and moist inside. Repeat with the remaining bread slices, 8 at a time. Set the toasted bread aside on a plate.

(continued)

2 long French baguettes

Extra-virgin olive oil

10 garlic cloves, peeled and smashed

2 cups (480 ml) fish stock, homemade (page 65) or good-quality store-bought

2 cups (480 ml) dry white wine

2 pounds (900 g) small fresh clams, cleaned (see page 64)

2 pounds (910 g) mussels, cleaned and debearded (page 64)

2 cups (300 g) red cherry tomatoes, halved

2 cups (300 g) yellow cherry tomatoes, halved

1 tablespoon red pepper flakes (optional)

1 cup (40 g) chopped fresh parsley, plus more for serving

Freshly ground black pepper

Salt

Heat 2 tablespoons of oil in a large saucepan over medium-high heat. Add the garlic and cook for about 5 minutes, until golden brown, stirring often so it doesn't burn. Raise the heat to high, add the stock, wine, clams, mussels, tomatoes, and red pepper flakes, if using, and bring to a boil. Cover and cook until the clams and mussels open, about 5 minutes, shaking the pan often (you may need to stir a couple of times to make sure you rotate all the clams and mussels from the bottom of the pan with the ones on top). Take care not to overcook, which will make the clams and mussels rubbery, and be sure to discard any mussels or clams that don't open. Add the parsley, season with pepper, then taste the broth and season with salt, as needed.

Place 2 slices of bread on the bottom of each of eight shallow bowls. Spoon some clams, mussels, tomatoes, and broth into the bowls. Top each serving with 2 more slices of bread and a sprinkle of parsley. Serve any extra bread alongside.

VARIATION

Spaghetti alla Pescatora: Cook the clams and mussels as above; when they have opened, remove them from the pan and set them aside in a bowl. Cook a box of spaghetti, and while it is still al dente, use tongs to transfer the spaghetti directly to the broth, tossing it well and cooking it for a couple of minutes to let it soak up some of the broth. Add a little more parsley, then place the clams and mussels on the bottom of the serving plates, top with the spaghetti, and serve.

LUCA'S TIPS: I personally love to eat cooked whole garlic cloves (you may have noticed the generous amounts I've used in my recipes so far!), but some people don't. If this is the case for you and your guests, use the cloves for flavoring and remove them before serving.

I like to use Vongole Veraci clams imported from Italy—they are on the small side and have a great flavor—but any variety will be fantastic here.

Fish Stock

Brodo di Pesce

Makes about 2½ quarts (2.5 L)

Heat the oil in a large stockpot over medium heat. Add the fish heads and bones and cook for 5 minutes, then add the leeks, onions, celery, carrots, and garlic and cook, stirring, for 5 minutes to soften the vegetables slightly and bring out the flavors of the aromatics. Add 2½ quarts (2.5 L) water, bring to a boil, then reduce the heat and simmer, uncovered, for 5 minutes. Skim off and discard any foam that rises to the surface. Reduce the heat to low, cover with foil, and cook at a bare simmer for 1 hour.

Strain the stock through a fine-mesh strainer into a large container. Discard the solids left in the strainer. If you're not using the stock right away, let it cool completely, then refrigerate until ready to use. It will keep for up to 3 days.

2 tablespoons extra-virgin olive oil

2 fish heads and bones (get these from your fish market when you buy a whole fish for filleting)

1 whole leek, cleaned well and roughly chopped

1 large white onion, cut into chunks

2 celery stalks, roughly chopped

1 carrot, roughly chopped

2 garlic cloves, peeled and smashed

FRIED MIXED SEAFOOD WITH MARINARA SAUCE

Fritto Misto con Salsa alla Marinara

2 tablespoons extra-virgin olive oil

6 garlic cloves, minced

1 (14.5-ounce/415-g) can chopped San Marzano tomatoes (with juice)

Salt and freshly ground black pepper

10 fresh basil leaves, julienned

1 quart (960 ml) vegetable or peanut oil, for frying

14 ounces (400 g) fresh squid, cleaned

Milk

6 unpeeled new potatoes

All-purpose flour, rice flour, or semolina flour

10 ounces (280 g) whitebait, very small sardines, or smelt, rinsed

¼ cup (10 g) chopped fresh parsley

2 lemons, cut into wedges

I'd never been a big fan of fried food, but in the past few years, I've discovered just how good fried food can be when it's done right, and nothing demonstrates the art of frying better than a good Italian *fritto misto* (see page 57 for tips on perfecting your frying). It's a dish you'd eat on the Adriatic coast and all over Italy, and I can't count how many plates of fritto misto I've served in the past decade working in Italian restaurants here in the States. It's a family-style dish—no need to worry about individual plating. Here I use squid, but you can also use shrimp, octopus, or even lobster, adjusting the frying time, as needed. I use the whitebait that are readily found all over the Adriatic coast, which in my region are called *bianchetti*, or "small white." If you can't find whitebait, you can use the smallest sardines available at the fish market or smelt.

Serves 4

Heat the olive oil in a medium saucepan over medium heat. Add the garlic and cook until lightly browned, about 2 minutes. Add 1 tablespoon water and let it sizzle. Add the tomatoes (with juice) and cook for 5 minutes. If the sauce is too thick, add a little water. Season with salt and pepper and remove from the heat. Add the basil. Set aside until ready to serve. Reheat just before serving.

In a deep-fryer or in a shallow saucepan over medium-high heat, heat the vegetable or peanut oil until a deep-fry thermometer registers 375°F (190°C). Line three baking sheets with paper towels.

While the oil is heating, prep the ingredients for frying. Rinse the squid and cut them in ½-inch (12-mm) rings. Put them in a bowl and pour in enough milk to cover them completely. This will help tenderize the squid. (You could do this several hours or even a day in advance; cover and refrigerate the squid in the milk until you're ready to fry.) Cut the potatoes into ⅛-inch (3-mm) slices.

Add the potatoes to the hot oil in batches and fry for 4 minutes, transferring each batch to one of the baking sheets with a slotted spoon and letting the oil come back up to temperature before adding the next batch. Repeat until all the potatoes have been fried.

Put some flour in a shallow bowl and season it with salt. Drain the milk from the squid rings and dredge the rings in the flour, shaking off any excess. It is important to start cooking the squid right after you dust them; otherwise they'll stick together. Place the squid in the oil in batches, adding them one at a time and making sure not to overcrowd the oil, and fry for about 5 minutes, until golden brown and crisp. Transfer each batch to one of the baking sheets with a slotted spoon and let the oil come back up to temperature before adding the next batch. Heavily salt the squid. Repeat until all the squid has been fried.

Dust the whitebait, sardines, or smelt in the flour, shaking off any excess, and place them in the oil in batches, adding them one at a time and making sure not to overcrowd the oil. Fry for about 5 minutes, until golden brown and crisp. Transfer each batch to one of the baking sheets with a slotted spoon and let the oil come back up to temperature before adding the next batch. Heavily salt the fish. Repeat until all the fish has been fried.

Working in batches, fry the potatoes a second time, until golden brown and crisp, about 4 minutes. As they are ready, return them to the baking sheet (you might want to set up a fresh layer of paper towels), pat off the excess oil from the top with paper towels, and heavily salt them. Let the oil come back to temperature before you add the next batch of potatoes.

Arrange the seafood and potatoes on a large oval plate and sprinkle with the parsley. Serve with the marinara sauce and the lemon wedges alongside.

The Calamari Challenge

The *MasterChef* Calamari Challenge pitted three contestants, Krissi, James, and Bri, against one another for the best fried squid. As I watched from upstairs, the first thing I saw they were doing wrong was adding eggs to the calamari batter.

Remember this: Italian fritto misto uses just flour, nothing else! If you see recipes for fried seafood that call for eggs, beer, or whatever else, that's a tempura batter, not a classic Italian fritto misto. The Italian way of frying seafood is about simplicity and elevating its natural flavor, not covering it up, so plain and simple flour, be it all-purpose flour, rice flour, or semolina for a little extra crunch, is, to me, the surest way to perfectly fry squid.

PRIMI

BUTTERNUT SQUASH SOUP WITH MASCARPONE AND LEMON-HONEY WALNUTS

70

BEAN, PANCETTA, AND RADICCHIO SOUP

74

SALMON, ROBIOLA, AND GRAPE RISOTTO

77

BEET AND GOAT CHEESE RISOTTO

80

ASPARAGUS AND LEMON RISOTTO

82

MUSHROOM AND BLACK TRUFFLE RISOTTO

86

SAUSAGE AND RADICCHIO RISOTTO

88

After the *antipasto* there is always a *primo*, or first course—small servings to accompany a multicourse meal. When I first moved to the States, the way risotto and pasta were presented in supersize servings was confusing to me. I believe that's where the misconception that risotto and pasta are fattening comes from.

In this chapter I focus on soups and risotto. The Italians and Italophiles out there may be wondering, *Where is the pasta?* Technically pasta is a primo, but as I have so many pasta recipes that are near and dear to me, I've dedicated a whole chapter to it (see pages 90 to 125).

In the pages that follow I'll show you how to make your own stock and share with you two of my favorite soup recipes, a fall butternut squash soup and my grandpa's favorite *fagiola* soup. And if you always wondered how to make a perfect risotto, this is the chapter for you! I'll teach you the technique for making a just-right al dente risotto and share some of my favorite ways of flavoring it up, with ingredients ranging from salmon and grapes, beets and goat cheese, asparagus and lemon, mushroom and truffle, to sausage and radicchio. Then you'll be well equipped to come up with your own signature risotto variations.

BUTTERNUT SQUASH SOUP WITH MASCARPONE AND LEMON-HONEY WALNUTS

Zuppa di Zucca e Mascarpone con Noci al Limone

I came up with this recipe for a church potluck one fall Sunday at the height of winter squash season. As the weather changes, I like to cook with butternut squash as much as possible: pureed, in soup, or stuffed into *mezzelune* and topped with crushed amaretti cookies (see the recipe on page 101). You don't necessarily have to use the mascarpone; it's a lighter soup without it, but if you're not on a diet, go ahead and enjoy it! For me, especially since my *MasterChef* experience, soup is never just soup: Multiple layers of taste and texture are called for, with the walnuts and croutons providing crunch and a flavor contrast to this creamy soup.

FOR THE WALNUTS

1 cup (120 g) walnut halves

2 tablespoons fresh lemon juice

1 tablespoon honey

Salt and freshly ground black pepper

FOR THE SOUP

1 (2-pound/910-g) butternut squash, peeled, halved, seeded, and cut into 1-inch (2.5-cm) cubes

8 garlic cloves, roughly chopped

1 large red onion, roughly chopped

3 sprigs fresh rosemary

3 sprigs fresh thyme

Salt and freshly ground black pepper

⅓ cup (75 ml) extra-virgin olive oil

2 cups (480 ml) vegetable stock, homemade (page 72) or good-quality store-bought, plus more as needed

8 ounces (225 g) imported Italian mascarpone cheese (such as Galbani or Polenghi), at room temperature

Fresh lemon juice

Serves 4

FIRST, WE'LL GET THE WALNUTS READY:
Preheat the oven to 325°F (165°C), and line a baking sheet with wax paper or parchment paper.

Place the nuts in a medium bowl. In a small bowl, whisk together the lemon juice and honey and season with salt and pepper. Pour the mixture over the nuts and toss to coat. Spread the nuts on the prepared baking sheet in a single layer and toast in the oven for 10 to 15 minutes, until they are nicely browned and glazed from the honey. Transfer to a plate in a single layer to cool, leaving the oven on. If they've stuck together after they've cooled, break them apart.

NOW WE'LL ROAST THE SQUASH:
Raise the oven temperature to 375°F (190°C), and line the baking sheet with a new sheet of wax paper or parchment paper.

Place the squash, garlic, and onions on the lined baking sheet and add the rosemary and thyme. Season heavily with salt and pepper, drizzle the oil on top, and toss everything together with your hands to coat. Cover the pan tightly with foil and bake for 45 to 60 minutes, until the squash is very soft. Remove from the oven and let cool. Leave the oven on.

MAKE THE CROUTONS:

Line a baking sheet with wax paper or parchment paper. Place the bread cubes on the sheet, drizzle it with a good amount of oil, and sprinkle with some salt and pepper and the rosemary. Bake for about 10 minutes, until golden brown and crisp. Remove and set aside.

GETTING BACK TO THE SQUASH:

Remove the thyme and rosemary and transfer the vegetables to a food processor, add the stock, and process until smooth with an even color throughout. Taste and season with salt and pepper, if needed. Transfer the pureed squash mixture to a large bowl and gently fold in the cheese with a spatula until fully incorporated. Add some more stock, if needed, to reach the desired consistency.

Place the soup in a large saucepan and warm it up over medium heat. Add just enough lemon juice to give the soup a little spark of brightness. Divide the soup among four soup bowls, sprinkle some croutons all around, and finish with some nuts in the center of each bowl.

LUCA'S TIP: I like to keep my mascarpone out of the food processor for this soup; it needs to be treated gently by simply folding it into the soup at the end. Anything more forceful can make the fat separate from the liquid, causing the soup to "break."

FOR THE CROUTONS

1 bread roll, preferably ciabatta, cut into crouton-size cubes

Extra-virgin olive oil

Salt and freshly ground black pepper

Handful of fresh rosemary leaves

Homemade Stock

Making your own stock at home may take some time, but it's very easy to do and allows you to know exactly what you are eating. Stock can be stored in the freezer for several months, so you can make a big batch, divide it among small containers, and use a little bit at a time in your recipes.

Vegetable Stock
Brodo Vegetale

2 tablespoons extra-virgin olive oil

1 whole leek, cleaned well and roughly chopped

1 large white onion, peeled and halved

2 celery stalks, roughly chopped

2 carrots, roughly chopped

4 garlic gloves, peeled and smashed

6 sprigs fresh thyme

2 sprigs fresh rosemary

Makes about 2½ quarts (2.5 L)

Heat the oil in a large stockpot over medium-high heat. Add the leeks, onions, celery, carrots, garlic, thyme, and rosemary and cook, stirring, for 5 minutes to soften the vegetables slightly and bring out the flavors of the aromatics. Add 3 quarts (3 L) water, bring to a boil, then reduce the heat to low, cover with foil, and cook at a bare simmer for 2 hours.

Strain the stock through a fine-mesh strainer into a large container. Discard the solids in the strainer. If you're not using the stock right away, let it cool completely, then refrigerate until ready to use. It will keep for up to 3 days.

Chicken Stock

Brodo di Pollo

Makes about 2½ quarts (2.5 L)

Heat the oil in a large stockpot over medium-high heat. Add the chicken bones and giblets and sear for about 4 minutes per side, until browned all over. Add the leeks, onions, celery, carrots, garlic, thyme, rosemary, and bay leaves and cook, stirring, for 5 minutes to lightly color them. Add 3 quarts (3 L) water, bring to a boil, then reduce the heat and simmer, uncovered, for 5 minutes. Skim off and discard any foam that rises to the surface. Reduce the heat to low, cover with foil, and cook at a bare simmer for 2 hours. Taste the stock to see if it's flavorful. If it's not yet full of flavor, cook it a little longer.

Line a strainer with a double layer of cheesecloth and place it over a large container. Remove the bones from the stock and strain the stock through the strainer into the container. Discard the solids left in the strainer. If you're not using the stock right away, let it cool completely, then refrigerate until ready to use. A layer of fat will form on top of the stock when it has cooled—you may want to remove it and perhaps use it in another recipe. The stock will keep for up to 3 days.

2 tablespoons extra-virgin olive oil

Bones and giblets of 1 chicken

1 whole leek, cleaned well and roughly chopped

1 large white onion, peeled and halved

2 celery stalks, roughly chopped

2 carrots, roughly chopped

4 garlic gloves, peeled and smashed

6 sprigs fresh thyme

2 sprigs fresh rosemary

2 bay leaves

BEAN, PANCETTA, AND RADICCHIO SOUP

Fagioli con Pancetta e Radicchio

1 pound (455 g) pancetta, sliced ½ inch (12 mm) thick

6 garlic cloves, roughly chopped

½ cup (20 g) fresh sage leaves

½ white onion, finely chopped

2 medium stalks celery, finely chopped

1 medium carrot, finely chopped

Salt and freshly ground black pepper

1 cup (240 ml) chicken stock, homemade (page 73) or good-quality store-bought, plus more as needed

1 (15-ounce/430-g) can red kidney beans, or 1¾ cups (375 g) freshly cooked red kidney beans

1 (15-ounce/430-g) can cannellini beans, or 1¾ cups (375 g) freshly cooked cannellini beans

1 cup (225 g) chopped canned San Marzano tomatoes (with juice)

½ head radicchio, chopped

Extra-virgin olive oil

This was a favorite of Nonno Velin, my mother's dad, with whom I spent a lot of time in the town of Casarsa, Friuli, as a kid. More often than not you'd find him sitting on a recliner next to the wood-burning stove with my grandmother cooking something delicious in the kitchen. You won't find this dish in any restaurant, because it's Nonno Velin's own unique way of putting beans, pancetta, and radicchio together in a bowl. My grandmother would cook the pancetta and beans and put them together for the soup and, as she often would, place a radicchio salad in the middle of the table. My grandfather would take the radicchio and stir it right into the soup. The soup would wilt the radicchio a little, but the radicchio still retained a good amount of crunch and lightened up an otherwise heavy soup.

If you are using dried beans, you'll need to soak them in water overnight and then boil them for a couple of hours. The last time I made this soup, I checked in with my mother, and while she was giving me pointers on putting it all together, I told her that I was using canned beans. "No, Luca, I can't believe the MasterChef is using canned beans!" Well, guys, no worries, I will not judge you if you do. I know we don't always have a lot of time for cooking, and with all the flavors that go into this dish, I promise you, no one will be able to tell the difference.

Serves 4

Heat a large sauté pan over medium-high heat until screaming hot. Cut the pancetta into rectangular bites measuring about ¾ by 1½ inches (2 by 4 cm) and add it to the pan. Sear it on one side until well browned, about 5 minutes, then turn it and sear it on the other side until well browned, 5 minutes more. Reduce the heat to medium-low and cook for about 10 minutes more to render the fat. (What we are doing here is getting all the fat out so you can cook the vegetables in it, and also crisping up the pancetta to use as a topping for the soup.) Taste the pancetta to see if it's nice and crunchy, then, using tongs, transfer it to a plate lined with paper towels. If there is more than ¼ cup (60 ml) rendered fat in the pan, pour the excess out and save it for another use, such as frying eggs.

(continued)

Raise the heat to medium, add the garlic and sage to the fat in the pan, and cook for 4 to 5 minutes, until the garlic starts to brown. Add the onions, celery, and carrots, raise the heat to high, and season with salt and pepper. Cook the vegetables until they start to caramelize, about 5 minutes, then add the stock and stir to release any browned bits from the bottom of the pan. Add the kidney beans, cannellini beans, and tomatoes (with juice) and cook for 5 minutes more to bring the flavors together.

Using an immersion blender, blend about half of the mixture in the pot, adding more chicken stock to the soup, if needed, to reach the desired consistency (I like mine pretty thick). Taste and season with more salt and pepper, if needed. Divide the soup among four soup bowl and top each with the radicchio and pancetta. Drizzle with some oil and serve, inviting your guests to mix everything together before they dig in.

VARIATION

Pasta Fagioli: Add a little more stock and a cup or so of cooked ditalini or any short pasta.

LUCA'S TIP: *Guanciale* can work in this recipe instead of the pancetta. Pancetta comes from the pig's belly (*pancia* in Italian means "belly") and guanciale comes from the jowl or cheek (*guancia* in Italian means "cheek"). Guanciale is really delicious, because it has even more fat than pancetta does!

SALMON, ROBIOLA, AND GRAPE RISOTTO

Risotto al Salmone, Robiola e Uva

My mother used to make us a delicious salmon risotto. The last time I mentioned it to her, though, she said she didn't remember it and denied ever making it. For the first time, my mother, the one I call more than anyone else, couldn't help me with a recipe! I turned to my *MasterChef* training: I would cook the salmon just briefly so it wouldn't dry out when I added it to the risotto, include grapes for something unexpected, and add chives and orange zest to play against the grapes and build up multiple layers of flavor. A little of my adopted home of New York City came into the mix, as in the end part of the inspiration for this recipe comes from the famous New York City smoked salmon and cream cheese bagel!

Robiola cheese is a very young, soft, and creamy cheese; you could also use mascarpone or any creamy cheese (yes, even cream cheese). When it comes to the fish, don't be cheap! Fresh wild salmon is the best choice. Yes, it is a bit more expensive than farm-raised, but there is huge difference in quality and flavor.

Serves 4

In a large saucepan, bring the stock to a simmer. Keep it at a low simmer while you make the risotto.

Heat 1 teaspoon of the oil in a medium sauté pan over medium-high heat until super-hot. Season the salmon cubes with salt and pepper and add them to the pan. Cook, without stirring, for 1 minute. Turn off the heat, add ½ cup (120 ml) of the stock and 1 teaspoon of the orange zest, stir to combine and release any stuck-on bits from the bottom of the pan, and set aside.

In a large saucepan over medium heat, melt 2 tablespoons of the butter in the remaining 1 tablespoon oil. Add the shallots and rice and toast the rice, stirring, for about 3 minutes, until the rice starts looking chalky. Add the wine, raise the heat to medium-high, and cook, stirring constantly, until the wine has been absorbed, about 5 minutes.

Add the liquid from the salmon pan, but don't add the salmon yet. Reduce the heat to medium.

(continued)

1 quart (960 ml) fish stock, homemade (page 65) or good-quality store-bought

1 tablespoon plus 1 teaspoon extra-virgin olive oil

12 ounces (340 g) fresh salmon, skinned and cut into ½-inch (12-mm) cubes

Salt and freshly ground black pepper

3 teaspoons finely grated orange zest

6 tablespoons (84 g) unsalted butter, at room temperature

1 large shallot, very finely chopped

1 cup (200 g) Arborio rice

1 cup (240 ml) white wine

½ cup (about 5 ounces/140 g) Robiola cheese or other soft creamy cheese, at room temperature

2 tablespoons finely chopped fresh chives

2 tablespoons finely chopped fresh parsley

½ cup (50 g) grated Grana Padano, at room temperature

1 cup (160 g) small seedless red grapes, halved

From here on, you will keep stirring and adding the hot stock 1 cup (240 ml) at a time, as the rice asks for it, waiting until the previous addition has been absorbed before adding the next. At the 10-minute mark, add the Robiola or similar cheese. Keep on stirring. Remember, the stirring is what makes your risotto super-creamy!

At the 17-minute mark, taste the rice. It should still be too al dente, but we are getting closer. Keep cooking, just a few minutes more, adding stock as needed, now in ½ cup (120 ml) increments, until the rice is just tender and creamy-looking but still al dente. The total cooking time will be about 20 minutes. Remove the rice from the heat. Add the salmon, the remaining 2 teaspoons of orange zest, the chives, and the parsley.

Now for the last but perhaps most important step: Cut the remaining 4 tablespoons (56 g) butter into chunks and add it to the risotto along with the Grana Padano; stir vigorously until the butter is melted, adding a little stock if it is looking too thick. Add the grapes, stir, season with salt and pepper, and serve immediately on flat plates.

BEET AND GOAT CHEESE RISOTTO

Risotto con Barbabietole e Caprino

2 (about 300 g total) red beets, scrubbed

1 cup (120 g) shelled pistachios

1 tablespoon extra-virgin olive oil, plus more for the pistachios

1 quart (960 ml) vegetable stock, homemade (page 72) or good-quality store-bought

3 tablespoons unsalted butter, at room temperature

Salt and freshly ground black pepper

1 large shallot, very finely chopped

1 cup (200 g) Arborio rice

1 cup (240 ml) white wine

1 cup (8 ounces/225 g) soft fresh goat cheese, at room temperature

¼ cup (25 g) freshly grated Grana Padano, at room temperature

¼ cup (10 g) chopped fresh chives

1 tablespoon apple-cider vinegar or white-wine vinegar

Beets and goat cheese is one of my favorite classic Italian combinations. I introduced you to the Beet, Goat Cheese, and Pistachio Crostini on page 22, so you know how well these two foods go together. This risotto is a lot of fun because the color is kind of shocking, like bubblegum. You would never think that something you'd eat for dinner would have such a fun color!

Serves 4

Bring a large pot of water to a boil. Add the beets, return the water to a boil, then reduce the heat to maintain a simmer. Simmer for 30 to 45 minutes, until tender. You can check for doneness by inserting a thin knife; if it goes in without resistance, the beet is done. Drain the beets and let them cool slightly. When cool enough to handle, peel the skin off using your fingers (wear disposable gloves if you want to avoid staining your hands), then roughly chop them. Place the beets in a blender and puree them, adding a small amount of water, if needed. Set aside while you start the risotto.

While the beets are still cooking, toast the pistachios. Preheat the oven to 375°F (190°C). Place the pistachios in a small bowl. Toss them with a drizzle of oil and a pinch of salt and pepper. Arrange the pistachios on a baking sheet and toast for 8 to 10 minutes, until lightly browned. Remove from the oven and transfer to a small plate to cool.

In a large saucepan, bring the stock to a simmer. Keep it at a low simmer while you make the risotto.

Melt 2 tablespoons of the butter in the oil in a large saucepan over medium heat. Add the shallots and rice and toast the rice, stirring, for about 3 minutes, until the rice starts looking chalky. Add the wine, raise the heat to medium-high, and cook, stirring constantly, until the wine has been absorbed, about 5 minutes. Reduce the heat to medium.

From here on, you will keep stirring and adding the hot stock 1 cup (240 ml) at a time, as the rice asks for it, waiting until the previous addition has been absorbed before adding the next. At the 10-minute mark, add the beet puree, then at the 15-minute mark, add the goat cheese. Keep on stirring to bring the starch out of the rice and get your risotto very creamy.

At the 17-minute mark, taste the rice. It should still be too al dente, but we are getting closer. Keep cooking, just a few minutes more, adding stock as needed in ½-cup (120-ml) increments, until the rice is just tender and creamy-looking but still al dente. The total cooking time will be about 20 minutes.

Remove from the heat, add the remaining 1 tablespoon butter, the Grana Padano, chives, and vinegar and stir vigorously, adding a little more stock if your risotto is looking too thick. When the butter and goat cheese are melted and incorporated, the risotto is ready. Add the toasted pistachios to the risotto before serving for a crunchy little garnish. Season with salt and pepper and serve immediately.

LUCA'S TIPS: If you're looking for another way to eat more beets and goat cheese, don't forget that the two make a great salad combo as well.

You can make more of the beet puree and use it to flavor and color a pot of mashed potatoes.

I LOVE CHEF GRAHAM!
He is a sweetheart, and somehow never harsh. In both my auditions, he said "no" to my dishes, but I am sure he was happy that I was able to prove him wrong.

ASPARAGUS AND LEMON RISOTTO

Risotto con Asparagi e Limone

1 bunch asparagus (about 14 ounces/400 g), woody ends trimmed and saved for stock

1 quart (960 ml) vegetable stock, homemade (page 72) or good-quality store-bought

7 tablespoons (100 g) unsalted butter, at room temperature

1 tablespoon extra-virgin olive oil

1 large shallot, very finely chopped

1 cup (200 g) Arborio rice

1 cup (240 ml) white wine

2 tablespoons finely grated lemon zest

1 cup (100 g) freshly grated Grana Padano, at room temperature

¼ cup (10 g) chopped fresh parsley

1 tablespoon fresh lemon juice

Salt and freshly ground black pepper

This is the first dish I cooked for my wife, Cate, and it's just like Cate: simple yet sophisticated. It's amazing how much flavor two everyday ingredients—asparagus and lemon—can bring to the plate. Cate loved this risotto so much that we went on to serve it at our wedding. At the time neither of us would have imagined that I'd be writing a cookbook with this recipe in it!

Serves 4

Fill a large bowl with ice and water to make an ice bath. Bring a large pot of water to a boil. Add the asparagus and cook for about 3 minutes, until slightly softened and bright green in color. Using a slotted spoon, transfer the asparagus to the prepared ice bath. Let cool for a minute, then, using a slotted spoon, remove the asparagus and pat it dry with a paper towel. Chop the asparagus into ½-inch (12-mm) pieces.

In a large saucepan, bring the stock to a simmer. Keep it at a low simmer while you make the risotto.

Melt 2 tablespoons of the butter in the oil in a large saucepan over medium heat. Add the shallots and rice and toast the rice, stirring, for about 3 minutes, until the rice starts looking chalky. Add the wine, raise the heat to medium-high, and cook, stirring constantly, until the wine has been absorbed, about 5 minutes. Reduce the heat to medium.

From here on, you will keep stirring and adding the hot stock 1 cup (240 ml) at a time, as the rice asks for it, waiting until the previous addition has been absorbed before adding the next. At the 5-minute mark, add the lemon zest; at the 10-minute mark, add the asparagus and 1 tablespoon of the remaining butter. Keep on stirring to bring the starch out of the rice and get your risotto very creamy.

(continued)

At the 17-minute mark, taste the rice. It should still be too al dente, but we are getting closer. Keep cooking, just a few minutes more, adding stock as needed in ½-cup (120-ml) increments, until the rice is just tender and creamy-looking but still al dente. The total cooking time will be about 20 minutes. Remove from the heat and add the remaining 4 tablespoons (56 g) butter (cut it into cubes first), the cheese, parsley, and lemon juice. Stir vigorously, adding a little more stock if it is looking too thick. When the butter is all melted, the risotto is ready. Season with salt and pepper and serve immediately.

VARIATION

Asparagus and Lemon Risotto with Shrimp: Flambé the shrimp as you would for the Seafood Soup on page 134. Remove the shrimp from the pan, chop it, and add it to the risotto after 15 minutes of cooking.

LUCA'S TIPS: It is important to blanch the asparagus in the boiling water for just a few minutes; you need it to keep a nice crunch, because you're going to be cooking it some more when it is added to the risotto.

Make sure to grate only the yellow part of the lemon peel; if you grate into the white pith, it can add a bitter taste to your dish.

MUSHROOM AND BLACK TRUFFLE RISOTTO

Risotto con Funghi e Tartufo

1 quart (960 ml) vegetable stock, homemade (page 72) or good-quality store-bought

6 tablespoons (84 g) unsalted butter, at room temperature

1 tablespoon extra-virgin olive oil

1 shallot, very finely chopped

1 cup (200 g) Arborio rice

1 cup (240 ml) white wine

4 tablespoons (60 ml) black truffle paste

½ recipe Sautéed Mixed Mushrooms (page 170)

Salt and freshly ground black pepper

1 cup (100 g) freshly grated Grana Padano, at room temperature

½ cup (20 g) chopped fresh parsley

Welcome to fall! Mushrooms and truffles are one of those things I wait for all year long.

Truffles are in the fungus family but are considered tubers rather than mushrooms because they grow underground. The truffle is a very fascinating ingredient, with both black and white varieties.

Let's talk about white truffles first: They have a very short season, from the end of October to the beginning of the new year, or at least that's the only time I would spend money on them, because that's when they are at their best. White truffles are a true delicacy; they can be sold for up to $2,200 per pound, and a restaurant plate of tagliolini with white truffles can go for $150. I did not grow up eating truffles, but I've been lucky enough to try this special dish a few times. Since white truffles are such a flavorful and delicate ingredient, they are most often used to finish a dish, as in the tagliolini or a simple Grana Padano risotto. Another classic dish is a simple fried egg with white truffle on top; I once added asparagus to the egg, and it was incredible! The most famous white truffles come from the city of Alba, in the Piedmont region in the northwest of Italy, so if you are ever around Italy at that time of the year, I suggest you make it a point to stop there.

Black truffles are far more affordable, and they have two seasons: summer and winter. The French have the edge on this one, as French black truffles are considered the best in the world. They are heartier than the white ones and can be matched with mushrooms and sauces as well as meat. Back in the day, truffle-seekers used to go around with pigs that would sniff out the truffles, but often the pigs would eat the truffles, so now dogs are trained to help do the job. Truffles grow next to the roots of trees and take on the flavor of the tree they grow next to. Pine, hazelnut, oak, and chestnut are some of the best. Truffles grow in just a few hours and only at night. A truffle-picker once told me that you could go to a tree at two in the morning and not find anything, and then go back to the same tree at six and pick a treasure. That might give you an idea of why they are so precious!

In a large saucepan, bring the stock to a simmer. Keep it at a low simmer while you make the risotto.

Melt 2 tablespoons of the butter in the oil in a large saucepan over medium heat. Add the shallots and rice and toast the rice, stirring, for about 3 minutes, until the rice starts looking chalky. Add the wine, raise the heat to medium-high, and cook, stirring constantly, until the wine has been absorbed, about 5 minutes. Reduce the heat to medium.

From here on, you will keep stirring and adding the hot stock 1 cup (240 ml) at a time, as the rice asks for it, waiting until the previous addition has been absorbed before adding the next. At the 5-minute mark, add the truffle paste; at the 12-minute mark, add the mushrooms and season very lightly with salt and pepper. Keep on stirring to bring the starch out of the rice and get your risotto very creamy.

At the 17-minute mark, taste the rice. It should still be too al dente, but we are getting closer. Keep cooking, just a few minutes more, adding stock as needed in ½-cup (120 ml) increments, until the rice is just tender and creamy-looking but still al dente. Total cooking time will be about 20 minutes.

Remove from the heat and add the remaining 4 tablespoons (56 g) butter (cut it into cubes first), the cheese, and the parsley. Stir vigorously, adding a little more stock if it is looking too thick. When the butter is all melted, the risotto is ready. Season with salt and pepper and serve immediately.

LUCA'S TIPS: Most of the truffle pastes on the market include mushrooms, and these are the ones I always use, because they are more affordable and full of flavor. When you are choosing a brand, make sure it contains 100 percent natural ingredients with little more than black truffles, mushrooms, and extra-virgin olive oil. You can find truffle paste in Italian groceries and international food shops.

Please stay away from anything that says truffle oil, as it is almost always something that is made in a laboratory and is not natural. It overpowers your dishes and can ruin your palate.

SAUSAGE AND RADICCHIO RISOTTO

Risotto Salsiccia e Radicchio

1 pound (455 g) pork sausage, cut into small pieces

Salt and freshly ground black pepper

1½ cups (360 ml) red wine

1 quart (960 ml) beef stock, homemade (opposite page) or good-quality store-bought

6 tablespoons (84 g) unsalted butter, at room temperature

1 tablespoon extra-virgin olive oil

1 shallot, very finely chopped

1 cup (200 g) Arborio rice

1 cup (100 g) freshly grated Grana Padano, at room temperature

2 cups (4 ounces/115 g) finely chopped radicchio (about ½ head)

½ cup (20 g) chopped fresh parsley

Red wine, sausage, and radicchio call for a cold winter day. This is another classic combination, one we've also used for the crostini on page 30. I hope that your butcher has some delicious homemade sausage for you; if he doesn't, you should consider a new butcher. A tasty sausage needs to have a nice blend of spices and, of course, a good amount of fat. Don't use ground pork for this recipe, as the recipe will never come out the same. You may be thinking that I should teach you how to create a great sausage blend, but if I give you everything in this book, I will have nothing left for my second one!

Serves 4

Heat a large sauté pan over medium-high heat. Add the sausage, season with salt and pepper, and cook until browned on all sides, about 10 minutes. Add ½ cup (120 ml) of the wine and stir to remove any browned bits from the bottom; cook until the wine has been absorbed, about 2 minutes. Remove from the heat and set aside.

In a large saucepan, bring the stock to a simmer. Keep it at a low simmer while you make the risotto.

Melt 2 tablespoons of the butter in the oil in a large saucepan over medium heat. Add the shallots and rice and toast the rice, stirring, for about 3 minutes, until the rice starts looking chalky. Add the remaining 1 cup (240 ml) wine, raise the heat to medium-high, and cook, stirring constantly, until the wine has been absorbed, about 5 minutes. Reduce the heat to medium.

From here on, you will keep stirring and adding the hot stock 1 cup (240 ml) at a time, as the rice asks for it, waiting until the previous addition has been absorbed before adding the next. At the 10-minute mark, add the sausage with its fat and any juices from the pan. Keep on stirring to bring the starch out of the rice and get your risotto very creamy.

At the 17-minute mark, taste the rice. It should still be too al dente, but we are getting closer. Keep cooking, just a few minutes more, adding stock as needed in ½-cup (120-ml) increments, until the rice is just tender and creamy-looking but still al dente. Total cooking time will be about 20 minutes.

Beef Stock

Brodo di Carne

Makes about 2 quarts (2 L)

Preheat the oven to 400°F (205°C).

Place the bones in a roasting pan and roast them for about 45 minutes, turning the pieces halfway through, until well browned. Remove from the oven.

Meanwhile, heat the oil in a large saucepan over medium heat. Add the leeks, onions, celery, carrots, and garlic and cook, stirring often, until caramelized, about 15 minutes. Add the beef bones, rosemary, and thyme and cook for 3 minutes more. Add 2½ quarts (2.5 L) water, raise the heat to medium-high, and bring to a simmer. Reduce the heat to low, cover the pan with aluminum foil, and cook at a bare simmer for at least 2 hours and up to 6 hours, occasionally skimming the fat and foam that rise to the surface of the stock (but don't stir the stock).

Line a fine-mesh strainer with a double layer of cheesecloth and place it over a large container. Remove the bones from the stock and strain the stock through the strainer into the container. Discard any solids left in the strainer. If you're not using the stock right away, let it cool completely, then refrigerate it until ready to use. A layer of fat will form on top of the stock—you may want to remove it and perhaps use it in another recipe. The stock will keep for up to 3 days.

2½ pounds (1.2 kg) meaty beef bones

2 tablespoons extra-virgin olive oil

1 whole leek, cleaned well and roughly chopped

1 large white onion, peeled and cut into chunks

2 celery stalks, roughly chopped

1 carrot, roughly chopped

2 garlic cloves, peeled and smashed

2 sprigs fresh rosemary

2 sprigs fresh thyme

Remove from the heat and add the remaining 4 tablespoons (56 g) butter (cut it into cubes first), the cheese, radicchio, and parsley. Stir vigorously, adding a little more stock if it looks too thick. When the butter is all melted and the radicchio is wilted, the risotto is ready. Season with salt and pepper and serve immediately.

PASTA

This is the chapter I am most excited about. My number one goal in writing this book is to teach all of America how simple it is to make homemade pasta. You might think that that's easy for me to say because, for sure, I grew up making pasta. Well, that would be wrong. My mother never made fresh pasta, and I don't remember ever making pasta with my grandmas either.

I do remember when I made pasta for the first time. It was in my apartment here in New York City, and the first thing I thought was: "Well, this is easy!"

Of course I grew up eating pasta, and so did and still do 99.9 percent of all Italians. It's part of our culture, tradition, and lifestyle. It's a major part of Mediterranean cuisine in general, which everyone knows is a very healthy way of eating. So please don't even start telling me how pasta is fattening, has too many carbs, and so on. My friends, it all depends on how much you eat. If you eat a pound of pasta at every meal, in a few weeks you'll look like a giant macaroni. If you eat modest amounts, it's not going to be a problem.

After I teach you how easy it is to make homemade fresh pasta, I'll show you how versatile it is by sharing some of my favorite pasta-based recipes. I'll take you into the *MasterChef* kitchen for my famous Broccoli Rabe Girasoli, then to my grandmother's kitchen with my favorite Christmas dish, Tortellini in Chicken Broth, then the Alps region in the fall with my Chestnut Pappardelle with Braised Veal, and the coast of the Adriatic Sea with the classic Linguine with Langoustines. For the finale I will treat you to my mother's lasagna, something you won't want to miss!

FRESH PASTA DOUGH

Pasta Fresca

Once you start making your own pasta dough, you may never go back to store-bought. Try it and see! I like to make my dough with extra egg yolks, because not only does it give me a nicer color but it also helps keep my dough soft. I don't really like to work the dough with my hands, so out of laziness and convenience I let my stand mixer work the dough for me. You can do the same or mix the dough in a bowl with a fork. Or you can be very old-fashioned and use your kitchen counter: Mound the flour on the counter, make a well in the center, and crack the eggs into it. Beat the eggs with a fork, gradually incorporating the flour into the well with the eggs, add the olive oil, and gather it all into a ball. When I make pasta this way, I always crack my eggs in a separate bowl to make sure I don't get any shell pieces in the flour mixture, and I whisk the eggs with the olive oil before I add them to the flour.

I keep my dough soft and elastic and then adjust it when I am working it in the pasta machine. If you keep your dough very soft, when you pass it through the pasta machine, not only will it stretch out, but also it will get a little wet again. So then you add a bit more flour for the next pass-through so the pasta will be smooth to the touch and not wet or sticky. If you start out with dry pasta dough, when you start rolling it in your pasta machine, it will crack and eventually break. Trust me, you'll get the hang of it!

3 cups (390 g) 00 flour (see sidebar), plus more as needed

4 or 5 large eggs

2 large egg yolks

1 tablespoon extra-virgin olive oil

Pinch of salt

The Great "00" Debate

There is a big debate about what flour you should use for pasta dough. In Italy, we use *farina* "00" (or *doppio zero*), but many recipes call for regular all-purpose flour. Why is 00 flour better than all-purpose flour? My good friend Jordan, who is American but has a great passion for Italian food and Italian culture in general, puts it this way: All-purpose flour is ground too coarsely for pasta; 00 is a finer grind. If you don't have 00 flour, he recommends mixing half all-purpose flour and half cake flour—all-purpose flour is too coarse, and cake flour is too fine, but when you mix the two, it all balances out.

Makes about 1½ pounds (680 g)

Place the flour in the bowl of a stand mixer fitted with the paddle attachment. In a small bowl, whisk 4 of the eggs, the egg yolks, oil, and salt. Add the egg mixture to the flour and beat on medium-low speed for about 30 seconds to combine the ingredients, then switch to the dough hook and mix on medium-low speed for about 2 minutes, just until a ball of dough forms, stopping the machine as needed to scrape any flour that sticks to the sides of the bowl. If you think that the pasta dough is getting too dry, you can mix in another egg; if the dough feels too wet and sticky, feel free to add a little bit more flour.

Sprinkle a work surface with flour and knead the dough for about 10 minutes, until it is springy, soft, and elastic. Cover the dough with plastic wrap and let it rest for 15 to 30 minutes at room temperature before rolling it out, or refrigerate it for up to 1 day; take it out of the refrigerator 1 hour before you are ready to roll it out, and let it rest, covered, at room temperature.

You Need to Knead

If you talk to any Italian grandmother, she'll tell you that kneading is the most important part of making fresh pasta. Kneading will stretch and warm the gluten and make the dough springy and elastic. The technique: Stretch out the pasta dough, pulling from the center to the outside and pressing with the palm of your hand. Then return the part that you just stretched back into the center. Repeat, turning the dough so you are not always pulling the same section. Only add flour if you need to, and be careful: If you add too much flour, the dough will get very dry. Put on some music and let your muscles go. Kneading can also be done by running the pasta dough through the pasta machine over and over again. You roll it out, then you fold it and roll it again until it is soft and elastic. With practice, you will be able to feel when the dough has been kneaded enough.

BROCCOLI RABE GIRASOLI

Girasoli con le Cime di Rapa

SPECIAL EQUIPMENT

Pastry bag or zip-top plastic bag, manual pasta rolling machine, pastry brush, 2½-inch (6-cm) flower-shaped cookie cutter

FOR THE FILLING

Salt

8 ounces (225 g) broccoli rabe, tough ends trimmed, chopped

2 teaspoons extra-virgin olive oil

2 garlic cloves, finely chopped

1 small shallot, finely chopped

Freshly ground black pepper

1 slice soft white sandwich bread, cut into tiny cubes

¼ cup (60 g) ricotta cheese, homemade (page 19) or good-quality store-bought

¼ cup (25 g) freshly grated Pecorino Romano

1 teaspoon finely grated lemon zest

¼ teaspoon freshly grated nutmeg

This is the dish I presented to the judges at the audition for my second year on *MasterChef*. They were kind of intrigued about the broccoli rabe. In Italy, broccoli rabe is usually served as a side dish sautéed with shallots, garlic, and red pepper flakes, not as a ravioli filling. I chose a pretty *girasoli* (which means "sunflower") shape for my ravioli and studied every component of the dish to make sure it was at its best when I got in front of the judges. Well, it wasn't, but it was good enough to get me a white apron, or maybe they just rewarded my boldness of presentation. I had to make the dish again in one of the final rounds to show the judges how far I'd come since that audition.

I improved the filling by adding lemon zest and going heavier on the seasonings, but I made a cheese sauce, and that was a mistake; the cheese congealed, and Chef Ramsay advised me to choose a simpler sauce that would accompany the ravioli, not overpower it. As soon as I came home from the show, I worked on it some more and perfected it, thanks to all I learned on *MasterChef*.

Making ravioli will take you a lot of time at the beginning, but when you get into the rhythm, you'll see how in the end it actually *saves* you time. I've included lots of extra pasta dough and filling, because who wants to do all that work for just one meal? Then you get to store all the extra ravioli in the freezer for a quick dinner whenever you like.

Serves 4, with lots of girasoli left over for you to freeze and cook up later (makes about 84 girasoli)

FIRST, WE'LL MAKE THE FILLING:
Fill a large bowl with ice and water to make an ice bath. Bring a large pot of salted water to a boil. Add the broccoli rabe to the boiling water and cook for about 5 minutes, until softened. Using a slotted spoon, transfer the broccoli rabe to the ice bath. Let cool for a minute, then drain.

Heat the oil in a large sauté pan over medium heat. Add the garlic and shallots and cook for about 3 minutes, until golden, then stir in the broccoli rabe and season with salt and pepper. Remove from the heat and let cool completely.

Transfer the cooled mixture to a food processor, add the bread, ricotta, Pecorino Romano, lemon zest, and nutmeg and process for about 30 seconds, scraping the sides once or twice, as needed, until smooth. Taste and adjust the salt and pepper, if needed. Spoon the filling into a pastry bag or into a zip-top plastic bag with one corner snipped off when you're ready to fill the girasoli.

ROLL OUT THE DOUGH AND FILL THE GIRASOLI:

Clamp your pasta machine to a long counter or worktable and dust the work surface with 00 flour. Divide the dough into four to six pieces (I recommend using smaller pieces if you are new to making fresh pasta). Working with one piece at a time and keeping the other pieces wrapped in plastic, dust the dough lightly in flour and flatten it a little with your hands, then set the machine to 1 (the thickest setting) and run the pasta through, adding a little more flour if it starts to stick. Set the machine to 2 and run the flattened dough through again. Repeat, setting the machine to progressively thinner settings (higher numbers), dusting with 00 flour as needed, until you reach the thinnest setting. When you get to the final level, dust your work surface with semolina flour to prevent the dough from sticking.

Fold the dough in half crosswise to find the halfway point, then carefully unfold it and return it to the counter. Brush half of the dough with some egg wash mixture. From the pastry bag or zip-top bag, squeeze out about 2-teaspoon mounds of filling for each girasoli, leaving about 1 inch (2.5 cm) between each mound on all sides. Fold the unfilled half of the pasta sheet over the mounds of filling and carefully press the two layers together to seal them, pressing around the mounds of filling and taking care to remove any air pockets.

Using a cookie cutter, press down and turn, centering the filling in the middle, to cut out flower-shaped ravioli. Place the cut girasoli on a parchment paper–lined baking sheet sprinkled with semolina flour, leaving a little space between each as you go. Sprinkle with additional semolina flour. Immediately transfer the baking sheet to the freezer. Begin rolling out and filling the remaining pieces of dough, one at a time. By the time you finish the next batch, the batch before it will be solid and ready to be popped into a freezer container or bag (if you were to place them straight into the bag before freezing them, they would stick together). Continue until you have run out of dough or filling. If you are completing the dish for tonight's dinner, reserve 28 girasoli on a baking sheet and cover them with a dampened dish towel.

(continued on page 100)

FOR THE PASTA

00 flour (see page 93)

1 recipe Fresh Pasta Dough (page 93)

Semolina flour

1 large egg beaten with 1 teaspoon water

FOR THE SALAD DRESSING

1 shallot, chopped

3 tablespoons white-wine vinegar

½ teaspoon Dijon mustard

6 tablespoons (90 ml) extra-virgin olive oil

FOR THE SAUCE

1 cup (240 ml) vegetable stock, homemade (page 72) or good-quality store-bought

4 tablespoons (56 g) unsalted butter

Salt and freshly ground black pepper

TO SERVE

8 teaspoons freshly grated Pecorino Romano

½ cup (20 g) microgreens, such as baby arugula

3 plum tomatoes, peeled, seeded, and finely chopped

¼ cup (30 g) toasted pine nuts

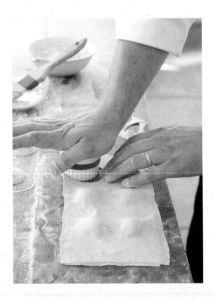

NOW WE'LL MAKE THE DRESSING FOR THE SALAD:
Combine the shallots, vinegar, and mustard in a blender and blend; with the machine running, add the oil in a thin stream and blend until emulsified. Set aside.

FINALLY, LET'S MAKE A SAUCE AND FINISH THE DISH:
Combine the stock and 2 tablespoons of the butter in a large sauté pan. Bring to a simmer over medium heat. Season with salt and pepper and turn off the heat.

Bring a large pot of salted water to a boil. Add the girasoli in batches and cook until they float to the top, about 1 minute (2 minutes if you are using frozen girasoli). As you cook the girasoli, turn the heat under the sauce to high and add the remaining 2 tablespoons of butter. As the girasoli are ready, use a slotted spoon to transfer them to the pan with the sauce. Cook, moving the pan around so the girasoli get an even coating of sauce, until the sauce has thickened a bit. Place 8 girasoli in each of four plates, placing 1 in the center and the other 7 all around it, making the shape of a sunflower. Finish each plate with 2 teaspoons of the grated cheese.

Quickly combine the microgreens, tomatoes, and pine nuts in a medium bowl. Lightly dress the salad with the dressing (reserve any remaining dressing for another use) and divide the salad among the plates. Serve immediately.

LUCA'S TIP: You can leave the salad out of this recipe if you'd like to make it easier, but the salad and dressing bring extra levels of flavor that make this what I consider a restaurant-quality dish.

BUTTERNUT SQUASH AND AMARETTI MEZZELUNE

Mezzelune di Zucca e Amaretti

Pumpkin ravioli in a butter and sage sauce is a typical dish from Friuli. I like to use butternut squash instead of pumpkin and add amaretto cookies for extra flavor, a little sweetness, and crunch. Italian grandmothers would tell you to mark the round side of the *mezzelune* (or "half-moon") with a fork, but I think it looks more modern without any marks. Making ravioli is a time investment, but you'll soon get really good at it, and at the end of your work, you'll have a freezer stocked with the makings of several great impromptu meals.

Serves 4, with lots of mezzelune left over for you to freeze and cook up later (makes about 96 mezzelune)

FIRST, WE'LL MAKE THE FILLING:

Preheat the oven to 325°F (165°C) and line a baking sheet with wax paper or parchment paper. Place the squash, garlic, and red onion on the lined baking sheet and add the rosemary and thyme. Season heavily with salt and pepper, drizzle the oil on top, and toss everything with your hands to coat. Cover the pan tightly with foil and bake for 40 to 50 minutes, until the squash is very soft. Remove from the oven and let cool. Remove the thyme and rosemary (don't worry if you don't get it all).

Place the baked vegetables in a food processor; add the bread crumbs, ricotta, and Grana Padano and process until smooth. Add the cookies and process to combine. Taste and adjust the salt and pepper, if needed. Let cool completely. (The filling can be made a day ahead and kept refrigerated. Remove from the refrigerator 1 hour before you are ready to fill your mezzelune.) Spoon the filling into a pastry bag or into a zip-top plastic bag with one corner snipped off when you're ready to fill the mezzelune.

ROLL OUT THE DOUGH AND FILL THE MEZZELUNE:

Clamp your pasta machine to a long counter or worktable and dust the work surface with 00 flour. Divide the dough into four to six pieces (I recommend using smaller pieces if you are new to making fresh pasta).

(continued)

SPECIAL EQUIPMENT

Pastry bag or zip-top plastic bag, manual pasta rolling machine, pastry brush, 3-inch (7.5-cm) round cookie cutter

FOR THE FILLING

1 (1½-pound/680-g) butternut squash, peeled, halved, seeded, and cut into 1-inch (2.5-cm) cubes

6 garlic cloves, roughly chopped

1 medium red onion, roughly chopped

2 sprigs fresh rosemary

2 sprigs fresh thyme

Salt and freshly ground black pepper

¼ cup (60 ml) extra-virgin olive oil

1 cup (120 g) panko bread crumbs

¼ cup (60 g) ricotta cheese, homemade (page 19) or good-quality store-bought

¼ cup (25 g) freshly grated Grana Padano

¼ cup (30 g) crushed amaretti cookies

(continued)

00 flour (see page 93)

1 recipe Fresh Pasta Dough
(page 93)

Semolina flour

1 large egg beaten with 1
teaspoon water

FOR THE SAUCE

½ cup (120 ml) vegetable stock,
homemade (page 72) or
good-quality store-bought

4 tablespoons (56 g) unsalted
butter

8 fresh sage leaves

Salt and freshly ground black
pepper

TO SERVE

4 teaspoons freshly grated
Grana Padano

4 teaspoons crushed amaretti
cookies

Working with one piece at a time and keeping the other pieces wrapped in plastic, dust the dough lightly in flour and flatten it a little with your hands, then set the machine to 1 (the thickest setting) and run the pasta through, adding a little more flour if it starts to stick. Set the machine to 2 and run the flattened dough through again. Repeat, setting the machine to progressively thinner settings (higher numbers), dusting with 00 flour as needed, until you reach the thinnest setting. When you get to the final level, dust your work surface with semolina flour to prevent it from sticking.

Line a baking sheet with parchment paper and generously sprinkle it with semolina flour. Lay the pasta-dough sheet flat on your work surface and brush the dough with some egg wash mixture. Using your cookie cutter as a guide, squeeze about 1-teaspoon mounds of filling into the middle of the cutter for each mezzeluna, then move the cookie cutter up the pasta sheet and repeat. Create another row of filling mounds alongside the first, again using the cookie cutter as a guide. Use the cutter to cut out the circles of dough with the filling in the middle. Fold one circle in half; if the edges of the dough don't stick together, brush them with some egg wash. Repeat with the remaining circles of dough, placing the sealed mezzelune on the baking sheet and leaving a little space between them as you go. Sprinkle them with additional semolina flour. Immediately transfer the baking sheet to the freezer. Begin rolling out and filling the remaining pieces of dough, one at a time. By the time you finish the next batch, the batch before it will be solid and ready to be popped into a freezer container or bag (if you were to place them straight into the bag before freezing them, they would stick together). Continue until you have run out of dough or filling. If you are completing the dish for tonight's dinner, leave 32 mezzelune on a baking sheet and cover with a dampened dish towel.

NOW WE'LL MAKE A SAUCE AND FINISH THE DISH:
Combine the stock, 2 tablespoons of the butter, and the sage in a large sauté pan. Bring to a simmer. Season with salt and pepper and turn off the heat.

Bring a large pot of salted water to a boil. Add the mezzelune in batches and cook until they float to the top, about 1 minute (2 minutes if you are using frozen mezzelune). As you cook the mezzelune, turn the heat under the sauce to high and add the remaining 2 tablespoons of butter. As the mezzelune are ready, use a slotted spoon to transfer them to the pan with the sauce. Cook, moving the pan around so the mezzelune get an even coating of sauce, until the sauce has thickened a bit. Place 8 mezzelune and 2 sage leaves apice on four plates, and sprinkle each plate with 1 teaspoon of the grated cheese and 1 teaspoon of the crushed cookies. Serve immediately.

MUSHROOM AND MASCARPONE QUADRATTI

Quadratti di Funghi e Mascarpone

SPECIAL EQUIPMENT

Pastry bag or zip-top bag, manual pasta rolling machine, pastry brush, pasta wheel with fluted edge

FOR THE FILLING

4 tablespoons (60 ml) extra-virgin olive oil

8 garlic cloves, peeled and smashed

2 shallots, very thinly sliced

1¾ pounds (800 g) mushrooms, sliced

4 sprigs fresh rosemary

4 sprigs fresh thyme

Salt and freshly ground black pepper

⅓ cup (13 g) finely chopped fresh parsley

4 slices (about 3 ounces/85 g) white sandwich bread, cubed

1 cup (230 g) imported Italian mascarpone cheese (such as Galbani or Polenghi), at room temperature

¼ cup (25 g) freshly grated Grana Padano

2 teaspoons fresh thyme leaves

When mushrooms are in season, I like to put them in just about everything. The delicious mushroom filling in this dish gets very creamy thanks to the addition of mascarpone. If you can't find mascarpone, you can use ricotta instead. You can use any type of mushrooms you like, and this isn't really the time to go all out with specialty wild mushrooms, as everything will be blended together in the end. *Quadratti* means "square," the shape of this ravioli; I use a pasta wheel to cut out my squares. Don't worry if they don't all look the same—that's the beauty of handmade pasta.

Serves 4, with lots of quadratti left over for you to freeze and cook up later (makes about 84 quadratti)

FIRST, WE'LL MAKE THE FILLING:

Heat 1 tablespoon of the olive oil in a large sauté pan over medium-high heat. Add the garlic and one-quarter of the shallots and cook for 2 minutes. Add one-quarter of the mushrooms, 1 rosemary sprig, and 1 thyme sprig and season with salt and pepper (the salt helps to release the moisture from the mushrooms). Sear the mushrooms, without moving them, for 2 to 3 minutes, until nicely browned on the underside. Turn the mushrooms and sauté for about 5 minutes more, until softened and nicely browned all over. Transfer the mushrooms to a baking sheet, keeping as much of the garlic in the pan as you can. Repeat the process for three more batches, transferring each batch to the baking sheet as it is finished. Remove the rosemary and thyme and return all the mushrooms to the pan; sauté until well softened, about 5 minutes. Add the parsley and remove from the heat. Let cool completely.

Measure out 1 cup of the mushrooms and set them aside for the sauce. Place the remaining mushrooms in a food processor. Add the bread, mascarpone, Grana Padano, and thyme leaves and process for about 30 seconds, until smooth with small flecks of mushroom showing. Taste and adjust the salt and pepper, if needed. (The filling can be made a day ahead and refrigerated. Remove it from the refrigerator 1 hour before you are ready to fill the quadratti.) Spoon the filling into a pastry bag or a zip-top plastic bag with one corner snipped off just before you're ready to fill the quadratti.

ROLL OUT THE DOUGH AND FILL THE QUADRATTI:

Clamp your pasta machine to a long counter or worktable and dust the work surface with 00 flour. Divide the dough into four to six pieces (I recommend using smaller pieces if you are new to making fresh pasta). Working with one piece at a time and keeping the other pieces wrapped in plastic, dust the dough lightly with flour and flatten it a little with your hands, then set the machine to 1 (the thickest setting) and run the pasta through, adding a little more flour if it starts to stick. Set the machine to 2 and run the flattened dough through again. Repeat, setting the machine to progressively thinner settings (higher numbers), dusting with 00 flour as needed, until you reach the thinnest setting. When you get to the final level, dust your work surface with semolina flour to prevent it from sticking.

Fold the dough in half crosswise to find the halfway point, then carefully unfold it and return it to the counter. Brush half of the dough with some egg wash mixture. From the pastry bag or zip-top bag, squeeze out about 2-teaspoon mounds of filling for each quadratti, leaving about 1 inch (2.5 cm) between each mound on all sides. Fold the other half of the pasta sheet over the filled side and carefully press the two layers together to seal them, pressing around the mounds of filling and taking care to remove any air pockets.

Using your pasta wheel, cut 2½-inch (6-cm) square quadratti, with the mounds of filling in the middle of each. Place the quadratti on a parchment paper–lined baking sheet generously sprinkled with semolina flour, leaving a little space between them as you go. Sprinkle with additional semolina flour. Immediately transfer the baking sheet to the freezer. Begin rolling out and filling the remaining pieces of dough, one at a time. By the time you finish the next batch, the batch before it will be solid and ready to be popped into a freezer container or bag (if you were to place them straight into the bag before freezing them, they would stick together). Continue until you have run out of dough or filling. If you are completing the dish for tonight's dinner, reserve 28 quadratti on a baking sheet and cover them with a dampened dish towel.

(continued)

FOR THE PASTA

00 flour (see page 93)

1 recipe Fresh Pasta Dough (page 93)

Semolina flour

1 large egg beaten with 1 teaspoon water

TO SERVE

1 cup (240 ml) vegetable stock, homemade (page 72) or good-quality store-bought

4 tablespoons (56 g) unsalted butter

3 sprigs fresh thyme

Salt and freshly ground black pepper

½ cup (20 g) chopped fresh parsley

8 teaspoons freshly grated Grana Padano

NOW WE'LL MAKE A SAUCE AND FINISH THE DISH:

Combine the stock, 2 tablespoons of the butter, and the thyme in a large sauté pan. Bring to a simmer over medium heat. Season with salt and pepper and reduce the heat to low.

Bring a large pot of salted water to a boil. Add the quadratti in batches and cook until they float to the top, about 1 minute (2 minutes if you are using frozen quadratti). As you are cook the quadratti, turn the heat under the sauce to high, add the remaining 2 tablespoons of butter, the reserved 1 cup of mushrooms, and the parsley. As the batches are ready, use a slotted spoon to transfer the quadratti to the pan with the sauce. Cook, moving the pan around so the quadratti get an even coating of sauce, until the sauce has thickened a bit. Place 7 quadratti on each of four plates, dividing the mushrooms evenly on top. Finish each plate with 2 teaspoons of cheese.

THE RESTAURANT TAKEOVER

Here I was assigned to the dreaded steamer to make scallop and shrimp dumplings in the heat of Chef Wolfgang Puck's WP24 kitchen in Los Angeles for forty-something guests. I survived, and we won the challenge.

TORTELLINI IN CHICKEN BROTH

Tortellini in Brodo

SPECIAL EQUIPMENT

Pastry bag or zip-top plastic bag, manual pasta rolling machine, pastry brush, pasta wheel with flat edge

FOR THE MEAT

8 ounces (225 g) oxtail

8 ounces (225 g) veal stew meat, cut into 2-inch (5-cm) pieces

Salt and freshly ground black pepper

2 teaspoons extra-virgin olive oil, plus more for brushing

1 white onion, finely chopped

1 large carrot, finely chopped

1 celery stalk, finely chopped

1 small leek, white and light green parts, finely chopped

4 garlic cloves, peeled and smashed

2 sprigs fresh rosemary

3 sprigs fresh thyme

2 bay leaves

1 cup (240 ml) red wine

1 cup (240 ml) chicken stock, homemade (page 73) or good-quality store-bought

2 tablespoons tomato paste

There is nothing that speaks to me more during the Christmas season than *tortellini in brodo*. Christmas Day was always spent at my grandparents' home: Nonna Anita would make the same favorite dishes every year, and tortellini was one of them. I started making tortellini myself for the first time just a few years ago. This dish takes some time, between braising the meat, cooking the chicken broth, and putting the tortellini together, but there are few things as rewarding as sitting down and eating a bowl of veal tortellini in chicken broth and knowing you made them with your own hands. You may just start your own holiday tradition!

Tortellini are usually served in chicken stock, but I will teach you how to make an elegant and clear chicken consommé. You will just need some chicken stock, cheesecloth, and egg whites. Of course, the tortellini can be served in regular chicken stock, but I like my broth to be as clear as possible for this special-occasion dish.

Serves 4, with lots of tortellini left over for you to freeze and cook up later (makes about 120 tortellini)

FIRST, WE'LL BRAISE THE MEAT:

Place the oxtail and veal on a baking sheet and season heavily with salt and pepper on both sides. Drizzle a little oil on top and brush it over the meat.

In a large saucepan, heat the 2 teaspoons of oil over medium-high heat until screaming hot. Add the meat and sear for about 5 minutes on each side, until browned all over.

Return the meat to the baking sheet, reduce the heat to medium, and add the onions, carrots, celery, leeks, and garlic to the saucepan. Season with salt and pepper and cook the vegetables, scraping the pan to release any browned bits from the bottom, for 8 to 10 minutes, until softened. Add the wine and cook for 5 minutes to reduce it.

Return the meat to the pan, add the rosemary, thyme, and bay leaves, and cook for 5 minutes, then add the stock, tomato paste, and 2 cups (480 ml) of warm water. Return to a simmer, reduce the heat to low, cover with foil, and cook at a low simmer, stirring occasionally, for about 2 hours, until the meat is fork-tender. It's ready when the meat comes off the bone by lightly pulling it apart with your hands and the juices have reduced to a thick sauce (the longer you braise, the more flavor the meat and sauce will have). If the sauce hasn't reduced fully, raise the heat to high and cook until the sauce has thickened and coats the meat well. Remove from the heat and cool completely. Remove the rosemary, thyme, and bay leaves and remove the meat from the bone. Taste and season with salt and pepper, if needed.

THEN WE'LL MAKE THE FILLING:

Place the braised meat and vegetables in a food processor and pulse to incorporate the ingredients. Transfer the mixture to a large bowl and add the bread, ricotta, Grana Padano, and parsley. Taste and add salt and pepper, if needed. (The filling can be made a day ahead and kept refrigerated. Remove it from the refrigerator 1 hour before you are ready to roll and fill your tortellini.) Spoon the filling into a pastry bag or a zip-top plastic bag with one corner snipped off when you are ready to fill the tortellini.

NEXT, WE'LL ROLL OUT THE DOUGH AND FILL THE TORTELLINI:

Clamp your pasta machine to a long counter or worktable and dust the work surface with 00 flour. Divide the dough into four to six pieces (I recommend using smaller pieces if you are new to making fresh pasta). Working with one piece at a time and keeping the other pieces wrapped in plastic, dust the dough lightly in flour and flatten it a little with your hands, then set the machine to 1 (the thickest setting) and run the pasta through, adding a little more flour if it starts to stick. Set the machine to 2 and run the flattened dough through again. Repeat, setting the machine to progressively thinner settings (higher numbers), dusting with 00 flour as needed, until you reach the thinnest level. When you get to the final level, dust your work surface with semolina flour to prevent the dough from sticking. Lay the sheet of dough out flat on your work surface and brush the dough with some egg wash mixture. From the pastry bag or zip-top bag, squeeze out two rows of about 1-teaspoon mounds of filling for each tortellini up the sheet of dough, leaving about 1¼ inch (3.2 cm) between them on all sides. Using the pasta wheel, cut lengthwise between the rows and then cut crosswise around the filling to make 2½-inch (6-cm) squares, with the filling in the center. Take a square and fold it into a triangle shape, pressing the top corners together and then sealing along the sides. Set the pocket of filling against the nail of your index finger with the peak of the triangle facing up, and wrap the two side corners around your finger. Press tightly to seal. If the two edges don't stick together, brush with a little egg wash. Place the shaped tortellini on a parchment paper–lined baking sheet sprinkled with semolina flour.

(continued)

FOR THE FILLING

1 slice crustless white bread, cut into very small cubes

¼ cup (60 g) ricotta cheese, homemade (page 19) or good-quality store-bought

2 tablespoons freshly grated Grana Padano

2 tablespoons finely chopped fresh parsley

Salt and freshly ground black pepper

FOR THE PASTA

00 flour (see page 93)

1 recipe Fresh Pasta Dough (page 93)

Semolina flour

1 large egg beaten with 1 teaspoon water

FOR THE BROTH

5 large egg whites

2 quarts (2 L) cold chicken stock, homemade (page 73) or good-quality store-bought

Salt and freshly ground black pepper

4 tablespoons very finely chopped fresh chives

4 teaspoons freshly grated Grana Padano

Sprinkle with additional semolina flour. Immediately transfer the baking sheet to the freezer. Begin rolling out and filling the remaining pieces of dough, one at a time. By the time you finish the next batch, the batch before it will be solid and ready to be popped into a freezer container or bag (if you were to place them straight into the bag before freezing them, they would stick together). Continue until you have run out of dough or filling. If you are completing the dish for tonight's dinner, remove 40 tortellini on a baking sheet and cover with a dampened dish towel.

NOW, WE'LL MAKE THE BROTH AND FINISH THE DISH:

In the bowl of a stand mixer fitted with the whisk attachment, beat the egg whites on high speed until they form stiff peaks. Line a large strainer with a double layer of cheesecloth and place it over a large saucepan. Scoop some of the whipped egg whites on top of the cheesecloth to cover the strainer. Very slowly pour the stock through the strainer over the egg whites. The egg whites will absorb all the impurities and some of the cloudy fat particles in the stock.

Repeat this process until you get the broth as clear as you like, using up the remaining egg whites. Or you can skip this step and simply heat up your chicken stock and proceed with the recipe.

Bring the broth to a boil and season it with salt and pepper. Lower the tortellini into the broth a few at a time with a slotted spoon. Stir occasionally to prevent the tortellini from sticking to the pan or each other and cook until they float to the top. As they are done, transfer them to four individual serving bowls with a slotted spoon, 10 tortellini to a bowl, then pour 2 cups (480 ml) of the broth over each portion. Sprinkle with the chives and cheese.

VARIATION

Cappelletti: Instead of cooking and serving your tortellini in chicken broth, cook them in boiling water, drain, and serve them in the butter and sage sauce that I use for my gnocchi recipe on page 116. Chicken broth is the most common way to serve this dish, but in some areas around Italy this is the preferred style.

LUCA'S TIP: Use the remaining egg yolks from the broth to make my grandmother's *zabaglione* on page 180.

CHESTNUT PAPPARDELLE WITH BRAISED VEAL

Pappardelle di Castagne con Vitello Brasato

FOR THE VEAL

1 pound (455 g) veal stew meat, cut into 2-inch (5-cm) pieces

1 pound (455 g) veal breast, cut into 2-inch (5-cm) pieces

1 pound (455 g) veal neck or other bones

Salt and freshly ground black pepper

2 tablespoons extra-virgin olive oil, plus more for brushing

2 white onions, finely chopped

1 cup (130 g) finely chopped carrots

1 cup (130 g) finely chopped celery

1 cup (115 g) finely chopped leeks, white and light green parts

6 garlic cloves, peeled and smashed

2 cups (480 ml) red wine

2 cups (480 ml) chicken stock, homemade (page 73) or good-quality store-bought

2 fresh rosemary sprigs

3 fresh thyme sprigs

2 bay leaves

1 (14.5-ounce/415-g) can chopped San Marzano tomatoes (with juice)

¼ cup (15 g) dried mushrooms, soaked in warm water to cover for 30 minutes and drained

This is the best pasta dish I've ever made. It calls for cold weather and red wine; it's something to make on a fall Sunday when the whole family is at home, the kids are playing outside, and the meat is slowly braising on the stove. Get a nice bottle of red wine for this meal.

Pappardelle is a very rustic type of pasta—that's why it is usually served with braised meat—so it is fine to keep it on the thick side. When you're making fresh pasta (especially when you're using new flours like the chestnut flour called for in this recipe) it is very important to understand how much flour you need to add to get the dough elastic and soft. It is a hard thing to teach, but a bit of practice will give you a feel for how it works. For this recipe, when you roll the pasta, don't be afraid to go hard with the flour. This will not be a filled pasta, so you can work it a little more, and it's OK if it's not as elastic as for the other recipes in this section.

Serves 6 to 8

FIRST, WE'LL BRAISE THE MEAT:

Place the meat on a baking sheet and season heavily with salt and pepper on both sides. Drizzle a little oil on top and brush it over the meat.

In a very large saucepan, heat the oil over medium-high heat until screaming hot. Add the veal neck or bones and sear for about 5 minutes on each side, until well browned. Return them to the baking sheet, add the veal stew meat and breast meat to the pan, and sear for about 5 minutes on each side, until nicely browned. Return the meat to the baking sheet.

Add a little more oil to the pan, reduce the heat to medium, and add the onions, carrots, celery, leeks, and garlic. Cook, scraping the pan to release any browned bits from the bottom, for 8 to 10 minutes, until the vegetables are softened.

Return the meat to the pan. Raise the heat to medium-high, add the wine, and cook for 5 minutes to reduce it, then add the stock, rosemary, thyme, and bay leaves. Return to a simmer and cook for 5 minutes, then add the tomatoes (with juice) and mushrooms. Cook for 5 minutes and season with salt and pepper. Reduce the heat to low, cover with foil, and cook at a low simmer, stirring occasionally, for about 3 hours, until the meat is fork-tender. Remove the rosemary, thyme, and bay leaves and discard them.

Place a fine-mesh strainer over a large bowl. Transfer the meat and vegetables with the braising liquid to the strainer, pressing on the solids with the back of a spoon to get out all the juices. Set the liquid aside and place the meat and vegetables on a baking sheet. Pull the meat apart into chunks, discarding any fat and cartilage that you find; it's OK if small bits remain. You can keep some or all of the vegetables. I like to keep about a third of the veggies, and definitely all of the garlic! Rinse the pan in which you braised the meat, return the meat and vegetables to the pan, and add a little of the reserved braising liquid; set aside the remaining braising liquid (you'll need more of it later to moisten the pasta). (The braise can be cooked a day ahead, cooled completely, and refrigerated. Reheat just before serving.)

NOW WE'LL ROLL THE PAPPARDELLE:
Clamp your pasta machine to a long counter or worktable and dust the work surface with 00 flour. Divide the dough into four to six pieces (I recommend using smaller pieces if you are new to making fresh pasta). Working with one piece at a time and keeping the other pieces wrapped in plastic, dust the dough lightly in flour and flatten it a little with your hands, then set the machine to 1 (the thickest setting) and run the pasta through, adding a little more flour if it starts to stick. Set the machine to 2 and run the flattened dough through again. Repeat, setting the machine to progressively thinner settings (higher numbers), dusting with 00 flour as needed, to the third thinnest level. Dust your work surface with semolina flour. Cut the dough into more or less 12-inch (30-cm) rectangles, then cut the rectangles into approximately 1½-inch (4-cm) strips to make pappardelle. Immediately place the pappardelle on a parchment paper–lined baking sheet generously dusted with semolina flour. Sprinkle with more semolina flour and cover with a damp dish towel. Repeat with the remaining pieces of dough, making sure to sprinkle every layer with semolina flour so the pappardelle don't stick to one another. Sticking is easily avoided, but if it does happen, you'll probably have to throw everything away, and that would be very sad! If you are not cooking the pappardelle, freeze them on the baking sheet, then transfer them to freezer containers for storage.

(continued)

FOR THE PAPPARDELLE

00 flour (see page 93)

1 batch Fresh Pasta Dough (page 93), made using half 00 flour and half chestnut flour

Semolina flour

TO SERVE

Salt

Extra-virgin olive oil

¼ cup (10 g) finely chopped fresh parsley

Freshly grated Grana Padano

AND NOW TO FINISH AND SERVE THE DISH:

Warm up the meat and vegetables, adding a little of the reserved braising liquid to coat it.

Bring a large pot of salted water to a boil. Quickly add the pappardelle one at a time in batches and cook for about 1 minute (2 minutes if you are using frozen pappardelle), until al dente, removing them with tongs and transferring them to the pan with the meat as they are cooked and returning the water to a boil before adding the next batch. Be careful, as they can overcook very quickly and break. Add more braising liquid to the pan with the meat, if needed, to give the pasta a good coating of sauce. Add a drizzle or two of oil and the parsley and spoon the pasta, meat, and vegetables into bowls. Serve sprinkled with the cheese.

LUCA'S TIPS: It is important that you don't overcrowd the pan when you sear the meat. If there is too much meat in the pot, the meat will release its juices rather than keep them in and will actually boil rather than sear.

Instead of veal neck or other bones, you can ask the butcher to save you the bones from the veal breast.

Chestnut flour may be hard to find, but Italian grocery stores often carry it through fall and winter. When you're making the pasta dough for this recipe, use half 00 flour and half chestnut flour. All the rest is the same. Chestnut flour can be very sweet, and it is often used in desserts; I cut the chestnut flour with 00 flour for the pasta dough so it doesn't get too sweet. If you can't find chestnut flour, using all 00 flour will be just fine.

You can cook any meat in this style. In Italy, pappardelle with wild boar is a very common dish; I also like to make it with lamb.

SPINACH GNOCCHI WITH SMOKED RICOTTA

Gnocchi di Spinaci con Ricotta Affumicata

FOR THE PUREE

2 cups (60 g) baby spinach leaves

Salt and freshly ground black pepper

¼ cup (60 ml) extra-virgin olive oil

FOR THE GNOCCHI

2 pounds (910 g) unpeeled potatoes

2 large eggs

1 teaspoon salt

1¾ cups (215 g) all-purpose flour, plus more as needed

¼ cup (25 g) freshly grated Grana Padano

FOR THE SAUCE

6 tablespoons (84 g) unsalted butter

Handful of fresh sage leaves

1 cup (240 ml) vegetable stock, homemade (page 72) or good-quality store-bought

Salt and freshly ground black pepper

TO SERVE

Chunk of smoked ricotta cheese, for finishing

Every time I go back to Friuli, I have to go into one of the *osterie* and order a plate of this very classic dish from my region. Gnocchi are the opposite of pasta in a way, as the gnocchi dough doesn't require any kneading.

You'll get used to making gnocchi once you try it a few times. The tricky thing about them is you can't know how they are going to turn out until you cook them. Some potatoes have more starch in them than others, so sometimes you may need less flour, but it can be hard to tell. The best thing to do is to try to use the same type of potatoes each time; if the first time you make them they don't feel as soft and light as you'd like, add less flour next time.

My dad loves this dish with smoked ricotta shaved on top; once you buy the cheese for this recipe, you can use any that's left over with any pasta dish.

Serves 4 to 6

FIRST, WE'LL MAKE THE PUREE:
Place the spinach in a blender and add a pinch of salt and pepper and 2 ice cubes. Run the blender and gradually add the oil through the hole in the top until the puree is nice and smooth. (You can pass it through a strainer into a bowl to make it even smoother, if you'd like.) Let stand.

NOW WE'LL MAKE THE GNOCCHI DOUGH:
Place the potatoes in a large saucepan and add cool water to cover. Bring the water to a boil over medium-high heat, then reduce the heat to maintain a simmer and cook for about 30 minutes, until softened. To test if your potatoes are cooked through, insert a knife into a potato. If it goes through without resistance, it is ready. Drain the potatoes, let cool just slightly, and peel while they are still hot.

Immediately pass the peeled potatoes through a food mill or potato ricer (it is important to do this when they are still hot!) into a large bowl. Make a well in the center of the mashed potatoes. Whisk the 2 eggs, pour them into the well, and work them into the potatoes with a fork or your hands. In a small bowl, combine the salt and flour, then work the mixture into the potatoes. Then work in the cheese. Last, add about

¼ cup (60 ml) of the spinach puree, a little at a time, and work it into the mixture until all the ingredients are incorporated and smooth. Add more spinach puree if the dough feels too dry; add more flour if the dough feels too wet. Form the dough into the shape of a bread loaf.

AND THEN WE'LL FORM THE GNOCCHI:

Line a baking sheet with parchment paper. Divide the gnocchi dough into six pieces. Roll each piece into a rope that is 1 inch (2.5 cm) thick.

Dust some flour onto your work surface, put the ropes on top as they are rolled, and dust the ropes with more flour. Then cut the ropes crosswise into gnocchi approximately 1 inch (2.5 cm) long. I like to make mine a little smaller; you can choose the size you like best. Dust the gnocchi with flour, then transfer them to the prepared baking sheet. (If you're not cooking your gnocchi right away, place the baking sheet in the freezer and leave it there until the gnocchi are frozen, about 1 hour, then transfer them to a freezer bag for storage.)

NEXT, START GETTING THE SAUCE READY:

Combine the butter and sage in a large sauté pan over medium heat and melt the butter. Add the stock, bring to a simmer, and cook for 5 minutes. Season with salt and pepper. Keep warm.

AND NOW, WE'LL COOK THE GNOCCHI:

Bring a large pot of salted water to a boil. Add the gnocchi in batches and cook until they float to the top, transferring them directly to the sauce with a slotted spoon as they are ready. Spoon the gnocchi and sauce onto plates and use a vegetable peeler to shave a generous amount of cheese over each serving.

VARIATION:

Arugula Gnocchi: Substitute an equal amount of arugula for the spinach.

LUCA'S TIP: If you cannot find smoked ricotta, you can use smoked mozzarella or any other smoked cheese. If you can't find *any* smoked cheese, you should reconsider where you are doing your shopping . . . but any aged cheese could work as well.

ORECCHIETTE WITH ZUCCHINI, RICOTTA, AND MINT

Orecchiette con Zucchine, Ricotta e Menta

Salt

1 (16-ounce/455-g) package orecchiette

3 tablespoons extra-virgin olive oil

1 shallot, very finely chopped

3 (about 1⅓ pounds/600 g total) zucchini, ends trimmed, cut in half lengthwise, and sliced into thin half-moons

Freshly ground black pepper

1 cup (240 g) ricotta cheese, homemade (page 19) or good-quality store-bought

⅔ cup (25 g) finely chopped fresh mint leaves

Freshly grated Grana Padano

The last time I was in Italy, I had lunch with my dad in a restaurant called Europa e Dintorni in Valvasone, the small town where my dad was born. The owner of the restaurant was my old friend Enzo. Enzo made his way up in the retail business; when I met him he was the general manager of a huge electronics store. When I applied for a job there, he and his fellow managers interviewed me, and I could see that the other people were not interested, but I got the job anyway. Within a few months, I was promoted to manager of the mobile-phone department, and Enzo told me that it was funny, as those other managers didn't really want me there in the first place because I didn't have a degree (I was nineteen and had just dropped out of high school).

A few years later, Enzo opened his first restaurant. Then he opened a second one just as I happened to take a trip back to Italy. He was looking for help. We worked together for more than eight months to build a restaurant that would go on to seat a full house for almost every lunch and dinner. Eventually, it was time for me to go. New York City was calling, but I will never forget Enzo, my mentor in business and life and one of the first people who believed in me. This dish is one of my favorites from the restaurant.

Serves 4

Bring a large pot of salted water to a boil. Add the orecchiette, and cook according to the package directions until al dente. Drain, reserving a small amount of the cooking water. Set aside.

Heat 2 tablespoons of the oil over medium-high heat. Add the shallots and zucchini and immediately season with salt and pepper (the salt will help the vegetables to release water). Cook, stirring often, until softened, about 5 minutes, adding some oil or water if you feel the pan is getting too dry, but remember—you want the zucchini to still have a bite, and adding too much water can cook it too fast and make it mushy.

Transfer the cooked pasta to the pan with the zucchini, add the remaining 1 tablespoon of oil and 2 tablespoons of the reserved pasta water and cook for 4 to 5 minutes, until almost all of the oil and water have been absorbed but the zucchini still has a bite. Add more pasta cooking water, if needed. Add the ricotta and mint and turn off the heat. Divide among four pasta bowls and sprinkle each with some Grana Padano.

LINGUINE WITH LANGOUSTINES

Linguine agli Scampi

One of my first *MasterChef* challenges was to cook a stunning dish with langoustines. If you watched the show, you know that it wasn't a success at all. Chef Gordon Ramsay even called me a one-trick pony because he said I could cook only pasta.

Langoustines are very tiny lobsters with a delicate and sweet taste. They mostly come from the North, Mediterranean, and Adriatic seas, so they are not easily available in the States. It's very hard for me to find them fresh, even here in New York City, so I'll usually buy them frozen from the fish store. This dish can often be found in restaurants on the Adriatic coast, especially in Venice and Trieste.

Serves 4

Place a langoustine on a work surface, belly facing down. Hold either side of the body with your thumb and forefinger and, using the tip of your knife, press down through the middle of the head to split it; continue to cut through the shell and entire body all the way through to cut the langoustine in half. Now we'll clean it. On the tail you'll see something that looks like a vein. Well, it's not a vein, and you don't want to eat it. Use the tip of your paring knife to pull it away. You'll also need to remove the guts, which are located just below the head; they are tiny and should pull right out with a toothpick. Then you will notice something greenish in color in the head that does not look very appetizing. This is politely known as the tomalley, also known as the brain. Just trust me that it has a lot of flavor and leave it be. Repeat the process with the remaining langoustines.

Bring a large pot of salted water to a boil. Add the linguine and cook until al dente. If the box says 11 minutes, I would take the pasta out at 9 minutes, as it will cook some more in the sauce. Drain the pasta and set aside.

Preheat the oven to 350°F (175°C).

(continued)

8 langoustines

Salt

1 pound (455 g) dried or fresh linguine

Freshly ground black pepper

3 tablespoons extra-virgin olive oil

4 garlic cloves, peeled and smashed

2 cups (300 g) cherry tomatoes, halved

⅔ cup (165 ml) brandy

2 cups (480 ml) fish stock, homemade (page 65) or good-quality store-bought, plus more as needed

1 (14.5-ounce/415-g) can crushed San Marzano tomatoes

1 cup (40 g) thinly sliced fresh basil leaves

2 tablespoons unsalted butter, cubed

A CHALLENGE AT THE CAMPGROUND

I had never gone camping in my life, so when the judges told us that we were going to spend the night out there, I was as excited as a kid at Christmas! Here I'm butchering pigeons with a Swiss Army knife.

Langoustines cook pretty fast, so this is how we're going to do it: Season the langoustines with salt and pepper and have them at the ready.

In a large sauté pan with a lid, heat 1½ tablespoons of the oil with the garlic over medium-high heat until screaming hot. Add half of the langoustines, meat-side down, and sear for about 3 minutes, until nicely browned on the underside (notice how the shells change color). Using tongs, transfer the langoustines to a baking sheet. Add the remaining 1½ tablespoons of oil to the sauté pan, then cook the remaining langoustines in the same way you cooked the first batch. Return the first batch of langoustines to the pan (keep the baking sheet handy; you'll be using it again soon), add the cherry tomatoes, and toss for about 1 minute, until the juices start to come out of the tomatoes and coat the langoustines.

Turn off the heat and add the brandy. Keep the pan lid nearby. Carefully ignite the brandy with a long kitchen match or a burning wooden skewer. (This is called flambé, and it gives an incredible flavor.) The alcohol should burn off in a few seconds, and the flames will extinguish. If they don't, quickly cover the pan with its lid. When the flames have subsided, return the heat to medium-high, add 1 cup (240 ml) of the stock, and bring to a simmer, scraping the pan to remove any browned bits from the bottom. Transfer the langoustines to the baking sheet you used earlier and set aside. (You're removing them so they don't overcook while the flavors come together in the sauce.) Stir in the crushed tomatoes (with juice), the remaining 1 cup (240 ml) stock, and the basil and season with salt and pepper. Bring to a simmer and cook for 20 minutes to thicken the sauce a little and bring the flavors together.

Place the langoustines in the oven to warm through for about 5 minutes while you finish the dish.

Drop the pasta into the sauce and add the butter. Using tongs, move the pasta around in the pan; grab some noodles and pull them up and then drop them. You are working to get the pasta well coated with the sauce. Add more stock if the pan is looking dry. Taste the sauce and adjust the salt and pepper, if needed. Place 4 langoustine halves on each of four plates, meat-side up, forming a circle with them. Using your tongs, grab some pasta, put it in the middle of the circle of langoustines, and do a quick turn of the wrist while dropping it to form a mound on the plate. Spoon the sauce on top of the pasta with a little on the langoustines as well. Serve immediately.

LUCA'S TIPS: When cooking pasta, it's very important that you move the pasta around in the water often to prevent sticking. Grab some noodles with tongs, pull them up, then release them back into the water; do this several times while the pasta is cooking.

Although I make this recipe with dry pasta (I usually use Barilla or De Cecco), of course it would also be great with fresh pasta. Now that you've learned to make pasta dough (see pages 93–113), you have the option of rolling out your dough and cutting out some linguine-, tagliolini-, or spaghetti-shaped pasta for this dish.

MY MOTHER'S LASAGNA

La Lasagna della Mamma

FOR THE BÉCHAMEL

2½ quarts (2.5 L) whole milk

2 whole cloves

½ onion, peeled

¾ cup (180 ml) clarified butter
(see page 125)

¾ cup (90 g) all-purpose flour

½ teaspoon freshly grated
nutmeg

1 teaspoon salt

½ teaspoon freshly ground
white pepper

FOR THE LASAGNA LAYERS

3 tablespoons extra-virgin
olive oil, plus more for drizzling

2 pounds (910 g) loose pork
sausage or ground pork

Salt and freshly ground black
pepper

¼ cup (60 ml) white wine

3 (13.75-ounce/390-g) cans
artichoke hearts, drained and
rinsed

¼ cup (10 g) thinly sliced fresh
basil leaves

1 pound (455 g) boxed or fresh
lasagna noodles

Softened butter, for brushing

1 pound (455 g) smoked
mozzarella cheese, cut into
small cubes

1½ cups (150 g) freshly grated
Grana Padano

The first time we ate this lasagna at home in Italy was just a few years ago at a huge family reunion with twenty people seated around the dinner table. I remember the expression on people's faces when we started digging in. I was almost surprised at how good it tasted. I've never been a big lasagna fan, but this one is something different. Cleaning and cutting artichokes can take some time, but I will tell you a secret if you promise you won't tell my mother: Here I use canned artichokes that I revive with some seasoning and fresh basil.

The key to a great lasagna is a great béchamel sauce. Béchamel is considered one of the mother sauces, so it's a good thing for any home cook to learn. Lasagna sheets are very easy to make (see the pasta dough recipe on page 93), but for this recipe, it's fine to use boxed pasta.

Serves 10 to 12

FIRST, WE'LL MAKE OUR BÉCHAMEL:

Pour the milk into a large saucepan. Stick the cloves into the onion and drop the onion into the milk. Bring the milk to a simmer over medium-high heat, watching carefully so it doesn't boil and stirring occasionally so it doesn't stick to the bottom and sides of the pan.

Place the clarified butter (see page 125) in a separate large saucepan, then add the flour a little at a time, stirring with a wooden spoon and making sure each addition is fully incorporated before you add the next. This paste is called a roux, and it's often used to thicken sauces quickly. Keep on stirring for about 10 minutes to get rid of that raw flour taste and to darken it a shade or two (this would be called a blonde roux).

Remove the onion with a slotted spoon and discard. Slowly whisk the milk into the roux; make sure you whisk vigorously to avoid forming lumps. Keep on cooking and whisking, reducing the heat a little if it starts bubbling too much and reaching all the way down into the pan to make sure the sauce doesn't stick to the bottom, until the sauce is smooth and velvety, 30 to 40 minutes. Remove from the heat. If you'd like a smoother sauce, you can pass it through a fine-mesh strainer or tamis, also known as a drum sieve. Add the nutmeg, salt, and pepper.

(continued)

NOW WE'LL GET ALL OUR COMPONENTS READY FOR LAYERING:

You can do this while your béchamel is cooking. In a large sauté pan, heat 1 tablespoon of the oil over medium-high heat, add the sausage or pork, and cook until the meat is seared on all sides, about 10 minutes. Season with salt and pepper, add the wine, and continue cooking for about 3 minutes, until the wine has been absorbed. Remove from the heat.

Cut the artichokes into quarters, squeeze them of excess water, then pat them with paper towels to absorb most of the remaining water. In a large sauté pan, heat the remaining 2 tablespoons of oil over medium-high heat. Add the artichokes and cook for 5 to 7 minutes, turning them just when they start to get golden brown (it's fine if they start to break up a bit). Stir in the basil. Add the sausage to the artichokes and cook together for 2 to 3 minutes to join the flavors. Remove from the heat and set aside.

THEN WE'LL COOK THE LASAGNA NOODLES:

Line a baking sheet with parchment paper. Bring a large pot of salted water to a boil. Add the noodles to the water in batches and cook according to the package directions (if you're using fresh lasagna noodles, you won't need to cook them). As the batches are ready, fish the noodles out one by one using tongs and lay them on the baking sheet; drizzle some oil between the noodles as you pile them on so they don't stick together.

NOW WE'RE READY TO ASSEMBLE AND BAKE THE LASAGNA:

Preheat the oven to 375°F (190°C). Brush a high-sided 9-by-13-inch (23-by-33-cm) baking pan with butter and place it on top of a baking sheet to catch any potential bubbly overflow. Brush a sheet of foil with butter as well.

Cover the bottom of the baking pan with a layer of noodles (you will be making three noodle layers total), overlapping the edges so there are no gaps in your base. Spoon half of the sausage mixture on top. Cover with half of the mozzarella, one-third of the Grana Padano, and one-third of the béchamel. Repeat with another layer of pasta, followed by the remaining artichoke-sausage mixture, the remaining smoked mozzarella cheese, one-third of the remaining Grana Padano, and one-third of the béchamel. Finish with a third and final layer of noodles and cover with the remaining béchamel. Top evenly with the remaining Grana Padano. Cover with the foil, butter-side down, and bake for 30 minutes, then remove the foil and bake for 15 to 20 minutes more, until browned on top and bubbly. Let sit for about 15 minutes before slicing and serving.

LUCA'S TIPS: If you're super-organized and happen to have two large sauté pans, you can start the artichokes while both the béchamel and sausage are cooking. If not, simply transfer the sausage to a bowl when it's done and cook your artichokes in the same pan.

If you're not using your béchamel right away, you can keep it warm in a bain-marie: Fill a large saucepan with 4 inches (10 cm) of water and bring to a simmer over medium-low heat. Place the béchamel in a heatproof bowl that fits into the pan snugly without touching the water, and place the bowl over the simmering water; stir occasionally until you're ready to assemble your lasagna.

If you can't find loose sausage, simply remove sausage from its casing before cooking.

Clarified Butter

When we clarify butter, we are removing the milk solids from the butterfat, leaving us with a clear golden fat that can be cooked to higher temperatures than regular butter. Clarified butter has many uses, particularly when it comes to sauce-making—it is used in such favorites as hollandaise and béarnaise. Also, clarified butter doesn't spoil as easily as ordinary butter, so you can keep it for quite a long time, up to three months in the refrigerator.

Gently melt two sticks of unsalted butter in a heavy-bottomed saucepan over low heat. The milk solids (the white residue) will separate and fall to the bottom of the pan, and foam will form on the surface (this is a mixture of some of the milk solids and the water from the butter boiling off). As the butter simmers, use a ladle to skim the foam from the surface of the liquefied butter. In a few minutes, you'll have skimmed off most of the milk solids, leaving just the pure yellow butterfat. Carefully pour the clarified butter into a storage container, being sure to leave behind any solids remaining at the bottom of the pan, cover, and refrigerate. Two sticks of butter will leave you with about ¾ cup (180 ml) clarified butter.

SECONDI

FRICO
129

PANCETTA-WRAPPED
SHRIMP WITH
ZUCCHINI PUREE
132

SEAFOOD SOUP
134

HERB-CRUSTED
BAKED MONKFISH
WITH EGGPLANT
CAPONATA
137

BRANZINO WITH
HEIRLOOM CHERRY
TOMATOES, FAVA
BEAN AND MINT
PUREE, AND
ASPARAGUS SAUCE
140

HALIBUT WITH
WHITE ASPARAGUS
RISOTTO
144

VENETIAN-STYLE
CALF'S LIVER
147

PANCETTA-WRAPPED
VEAL CUTLET WITH
RADICCHIO, APPLES,
AND WHITE-WINE
SAUCE
150

COTECHINO WITH
SAUERKRAUT
155

MY MOTHER'S
MEATBALLS
158

RACK OF LAMB WITH
POTATO PUREE
160

NEW YORK STRIP
STEAK WITH
VANILLA SAUCE
162

BRAISED BEEF
SHORT RIBS WITH
CHANTERELLES AND
SUNCHOKE PUREE
164

Il secondo for me is the most important course of the meal. The main course is what can make or break a dinner. If your appetizer is just OK but the main course blows you away, you will have a great memory of that meal. If the appetizer was awesome but the main course was disappointing, most likely that dinner will leave you with a bitter taste.

I try to keep food choices cohesive for my meals; a seafood or fish *primo* calls for a seafood or fish main course, with white wine most of the time, and a meat *primo* calls for a meat main course and red wine.

This chapter showcases a variety of dishes; there are a few very homey and traditional dishes, a few *MasterChef* classics, and some restaurant-quality recipes that will amaze your guests. You'll learn how to make *frico*, a classic potato and cheese dish from my region of Friuli, and *cotechino*, the most traditional dish of my Christmas holidays. The vanilla steak and rack of lamb will leave your friends speechless, and when you make the halibut and my famous short ribs (the ones that helped me win the competition), you will feel like you are in the *MasterChef* kitchen cooking with me.

FRICO

America, meet frico! I was so excited when I got to cook this dish in the *MasterChef* finals (see page 150 for the story on how this Italian got to cook cheese), as it gave me the honor of paying tribute to my roots on national television. Frico represents where I come from, as it's one of the most traditional dishes of Friuli. If I don't name my first restaurant Luca, I just might call it Frico. It's a humble and simple dish, like the people of Friuli; it's made with potatoes, onions, and cheese—all ingredients that were and still are never missing from any kitchen in that area. It can be served as a main course or as an accompaniment to a meal. Traditionally it is served with polenta—plain, creamy, or grilled.

Frico is traditionally made with Montasio cheese, which is an important cheese in the cuisine of Friuli, but that does not mean you can't use other cheeses instead. You just need a young cheese, one that is not aged more than three months, and a second cheese that is aged for more than six months. Avoid any cheese with a bite in it such as blue cheese and creamy cheeses; mild-flavored cheeses work best. You might use Piave or Asiago if you cannot find Montasio. On *MasterChef* I had to use Grana Padano, which is the king of Italian cheeses, and I matched it with a very young Gruyère. It doesn't sound as if it would be the best combination, but it actually worked. These are two cheeses you could easily find at the supermarket.

I would not suggest serving this dish in the middle of summer, as you would probably melt like the cheese inside it. This is a fall/winter dish that needs to be served with lots and lots of red wine—even better if the wine is from Friuli.

2 tablespoons extra-virgin olive oil

2 white onions, very thinly sliced

Salt and freshly ground black pepper

1 pound (455 g) russet or Yukon Gold potatoes, peeled

8 ounces (225 g) young Montasio cheese, cut into small cubes

8 ounces (225 g) aged Montasio cheese, cut into small cubes

Serves 4 to 6

Bring a small pot of water to a slow simmer over low heat and keep it warm.

Heat the oil in a large nonstick pan over medium-low heat. Add the onions, season with salt and pepper, and cook for 20 to 30 minutes, until the onions are very soft, taking care not to let them get caramelized and adding a little hot water if the pan starts to get dry.

(continued)

First, raise the heat to medium. This is where it gets a little tricky: Using the large holes of a box grater, grate the potatoes right into the pan with the onion (if that seems a little daunting, quickly grate them into a bowl and add them to the pan all at once). Using two wooden spoons, work the potatoes and onions together until they are fully incorporated into a very sticky and wet paste; this will take about 5 minutes. Work that paste! We want to make it as homogenous as possible.

Add the cheeses to the potato mixture. Using the two wooden spoons, work the mixture—grabbing it, lifting it up, stretching it, and repeating—until all the cheese is melted and incorporated and you have a uniform paste; this will take about 5 minutes.

Smooth the mixture into an even layer to cover the pan's bottom and cook until lightly browned on the bottom, 5 to 10 minutes (use a spatula to lift and check on the color of the bottom crust). Place a large round plate upside down on top of the pan. Turn off the heat, then very rapidly invert the pan and the plate together so the frico ends up on the plate. Set the pan back on the stove, slide the frico back into the pan, and turn the heat to medium-low. Continue to cook until a light brown crust forms on the bottom, 5 to 10 minutes.

I suggest serving this classic on a large wooden tray or even a cutting board.

LUCA'S TIPS: Three simple but very important steps will give you a perfect frico: 1) Cook down the onions very slowly; 2) Grate the potatoes—don't cut, chop, or shave them; and 3) Most important, you absolutely need a nonstick pan to get that all-important crust. Don't even waste your time if your nonstick is old and scratched—it will be impossible to flip your frico. It just won't work!

PANCETTA-WRAPPED SHRIMP WITH ZUCCHINI PUREE

Gamberoni con Pancetta e Puree di Zucchine

24 very thin slices pancetta

12 jumbo shrimp, peeled but with the tail left on

1 large potato, peeled and cut into cubes

1 tablespoon unsalted butter

1 cup (115 g) very finely chopped leek, white and light green parts

2 zucchini (about 10 ounces/ 280 g), finely chopped

Salt and freshly ground black pepper

¾ to 1 cup (180 to 240 ml) vegetable stock, homemade (page 72) or good-quality store-bought

2 tablespoons chopped fresh mint leaves

1 tablespoon chopped fresh tarragon

1 tablespoon extra-virgin olive oil, plus more as needed

Whenever you go to a seafood restaurant on the Adriatic coast, you will find a grilled *gamberoni* (shrimp) dish on the menu. My shrimp, wrapped in pancetta and served over a zucchini puree, kicks this standard up a notch. If you're ever in an authentic Italian butcher shop, look for *lardo di colonnata* and give it a try; this type of cured fatback is even fattier than pancetta and is simply amazing.

Serves 4

Place 2 slices of pancetta on a work surface, place a shrimp on top, and wrap the shrimp in the pancetta (you may need to overlap the pancetta depending on how big your shrimp are); give it a little squeeze to seal it. Place on a plate and repeat with the remaining shrimp and pancetta. Refrigerate.

Bring a small saucepan of water to a boil over high heat. Add the potatoes, reduce the heat, and simmer until softened, about 10 minutes. Drain.

Meanwhile, melt the butter in a large sauté pan over low heat. Add the leeks and cook for 5 minutes, or until softened, then add the zucchini, season with salt and pepper, and cook for 5 to 7 minutes more, until the zucchini is softened. Add the potatoes and ¾ cup (180 ml) stock, cover, and bring to a simmer. Turn off the heat, transfer to a food processor or blender, and process until smooth, adding more stock through the hole in the top, if needed, to make a very smooth puree. Season with salt and pepper, add the mint and tarragon, and process to combine. At the very end, with the machine still running, drizzle in the olive oil and then immediately stop the machine—this will give your puree a nice sheen. Return the puree to the pan and keep warm until ready to serve.

Heat a drizzle of oil in a large sauté pan until screaming hot. Add 6 of the pancetta-wrapped shrimp and sear until the bottom is golden brown, about 90 seconds. Remove the pan from the heat, quickly flip the shrimp using tongs, return the pan to the heat, and sear until the second side is golden brown and the shrimp turn pink, another 90 seconds or so. Transfer the shrimp to a plate. Repeat with the remaining 6 shrimp. Return the first batch of shrimp to the pan, reduce the heat to low, cover, and cook for 2 minutes more.

Spoon the zucchini puree into the center of each of four plates and top each plate with 3 shrimp. Serve immediately.

VARIATIONS

You can use any type of white-fleshed fish, such as cod or halibut, instead of the shrimp. Cut the fish into pieces and wrap them the same way you'd wrap the shrimp. If you are wrapping the fish in pancetta, sear it the way you did for the shrimp and finish it in the oven for about 3 minutes at 375°F (190°C).

LUCA'S TIPS: You can turn the zucchini puree into a soup by adding some vegetable stock to thin it a little.

If you are using lardo di colonnata, make the entire recipe in the oven, baking it for about 5 minutes at 375°F (190°C) so the lard will completely melt into the fish.

Wrapping It Up with Pancetta

In case you haven't noticed, I love pancetta, and I also love to wrap food in it! It's a very simple thing to do, and the flavor of any food goes through the roof when you wrap it in pancetta. Pancetta can be very delicate, and it's almost impossible to slice at home, so please have your butcher do it for you. If you find the pancetta is hard to handle and starts to tear, try freezing it for about 30 minutes before wrapping, then refrigerate the food you've just wrapped until it's ready to go into the pan. (This isn't something I would do in my kitchen, but if you're new to pancetta wrapping, it can make things easier for you.) This allows the pancetta to melt right into the food, which will make your taste buds very happy and get you plotting how to wrap other foods in pancetta!

SEAFOOD SOUP

Brodetto di Pesce

FOR THE OCTOPUS

2 tablespoons extra-virgin olive oil

1 cup very finely chopped celery

⅔ cup (75 g) finely chopped leeks, white parts only

⅔ cup (70 g) finely chopped shallots

4 garlic cloves, peeled and smashed

4 baby octopus

Salt and freshly ground black pepper

⅔ cup (120 g) pitted green olives

2 tablespoons capers, drained and rinsed

1 (28-ounce/795-g) can chopped San Marzano tomatoes (with juice)

1 cup (40 g) thinly sliced fresh basil leaves

FOR THE SHRIMP

8 head-on jumbo shrimp, peeled but with tail left on, and deveined

Salt and freshly ground black pepper

2 tablespoons extra-virgin olive oil

4 garlic cloves, peeled and smashed

(continued)

For our anniversary, my wife, Cate, and I treated ourselves to a meal at a restaurant here in New York City called Marea. It's the restaurant where Cate, my best man, and I went for lunch after Cate and I eloped. Marea is Chef Michael White's modern Italian seafood restaurant, and it earned him two Michelin stars. It is my favorite restaurant in Manhattan. The last time we went there, I had a phenomenal *brodetto di pesce*, a classic seafood soup with a brandy broth and toasted ciabatta. I ate it very slowly because I did not want it to be over, and that soup was my inspiration for this recipe. It's a pretty long recipe, but the individual steps are easy, and the final result is incredible.

You could be served this dish anywhere along the coast of Italy, from the Adriatic to the Amalfi coast. You'll need some seafood stock for it, so when you buy your red snapper, ask the fish guy to clean and fillet them for you and bring the bones home to make a stock. I love to season my fish with a flavored salt, like black or red salt, and I particularly love smoky salt for the snapper. For something really different, I use a salt infused with lavender and oranges. But I leave it to you to get creative with your seasonings so you can give the soup your own personal touch.

Serves 4

MAKE THE OCTOPUS:

In a medium saucepan, heat the oil over medium heat. Add the celery, leeks, shallots, and garlic and cook for about 5 minutes, until softened; add a little water if the pan starts to get dry. Season the octopus with salt and pepper, add it to the pan, and cook for 5 minutes to begin to soften it. Add the olives and capers and cook for 2 minutes more. Add the tomatoes (with juice), basil, and 1 cup (240 ml) of water. Bring to a boil, then reduce the heat to low, cover with foil, and cook for about 45 minutes, until the octopus is tender. Using tongs, remove the octopus from the sauce and place it in a bowl. Grab a fine-mesh strainer and set it over a large bowl. Strain the sauce into the bowl; use the back of a spoon to push all the juices out. The result will be a clear reddish liquid (discard any solids in the strainer). This is the base for your broth.

MEANWHILE, WE'LL MAKE THE SHRIMP:

Season the shrimp with salt and pepper. In a large sauté pan, heat the oil with the garlic and thyme over medium-high heat. When the pan is screaming hot, add the shrimp and sear them for 2 minutes or so, until they are nicely browned on the bottom (turn one to check). Turn the shrimp, add the brandy, and turn off the heat. With the lid to the pan nearby, carefully ignite the brandy with a long kitchen match or a burning wooden skewer. (This is called flambé, and it gives an incredible flavor.) The alcohol should burn off in a few seconds, and the flames will extinguish. If they don't, quickly cover the pan with its lid. When the flames have subsided, transfer the shrimp to a plate. Turn the heat back to medium-high, add the stock to the pan with the shrimp cooking juices, and cook for 2 minutes, scraping the pan to remove any browned bits from the bottom. Strain the cooking liquid into a medium bowl and set aside. Discard any solids left in the strainer.

LET'S MOVE TO THE CLAMS AND MUSSELS:

Rinse and dry the sauté pan in which you cooked the shrimp. Add the oil and garlic and heat over medium-high heat until screaming hot. Add the clams, mussels, wine, stock, and parsley. Cover and cook, shaking the pan often, just until the clams and mussels open, about 3 minutes. Discard any clams or mussels that don't open. Transfer the clams and mussels to a medium bowl. Cook the pan liquids for about 2 minutes to concentrate the flavors. Strain the clam and mussel cooking liquid into the bowl containing the shrimp cooking liquid. Discard any solids left in the strainer.

AND TO CRISP UP THE BAGUETTE:

Rinse and dry the sauté pan in which you cooked the clams and mussels. Cut 4 small (1-by-4-inch/2.5-by-10-cm) and 4 large (1-by-7-inch/2.5-by-17-cm) slices from the baguette. In a large sauté pan, heat 1 tablespoon of oil over medium-high heat. Arrange as many bread slices in the pan as can fit and toast for about 5 minutes, until golden brown and crisp. Sprinkle another tablespoon of oil over the top of the bread slices, then flip them and toast until golden brown and crisp on the second side, about 5 minutes more. The idea is to soak the bread in oil, then crisp it up on the outside so the bread is crunchy outside and nice and moist inside. Transfer to a plate and repeat with the remaining bread.

(continued)

2 sprigs fresh thyme

½ cup (120 ml) brandy

½ cup (120 ml) fish stock, homemade (page 65) or good-quality store-bought

FOR THE CLAMS AND MUSSELS

2 tablespoons extra-virgin olive oil

2 garlic cloves

1 pound (455 g) clams, cleaned (see page 64)

1 pound (455 g) mussels, cleaned and debearded (see page 64)

1 cup (240 ml) white wine

½ cup (120 ml) fish stock, homemade (page 65) or good-quality store-bought

½ cup (20 g) chopped fresh parsley

FOR THE TOASTED BAGUETTE

1 large baguette

Extra-virgin olive oil

FOR THE SEAFOOD BROTH

1 tablespoon red pepper flakes (optional)

FOR THE RED SNAPPER

4 (4-ounce/115-g) skin-on red snapper fillets

Sea salt or flavored salt

2 tablespoons extra-virgin olive oil

2 sprigs fresh rosemary

NOW WE'LL MAKE THE FISH:

Score the fish a few times with a knife; I like to trim the narrow part of the fillet to pretty up my presentation. Season with sea salt or flavored salt. In a large sauté pan, heat the oil over medium-high heat until screaming hot. Add the rosemary, then add the fish to the pan, skin-side down, pressing a few times on the fillets with a spatula for the first 30 seconds to prevent the fish from curling. Cook until 90 percent cooked through, about 3 minutes. Quickly flip the fish and cook for about 20 seconds more, until the fish is just cooked through (keep in mind that it will cook a little more when it gets topped with the broth). Remove from the heat.

FINALLY, WE'LL FINISH OUR BROTH:

While the fish is cooking, in a medium saucepan, combine the shrimp, clam, and mussel cooking liquid with the octopus cooking liquid. Set over medium heat, bring to a simmer, and cook for 2 to 3 minutes to combine the flavors. Taste for seasoning and add some more salt, if needed, and the red pepper flakes, if you like it spicy. I personally don't, but I won't disagree with you if you do.

AND TO SERVE:

Add the octopus, shrimp, clams, and mussels to the seafood broth and heat just enough to warm them all up. Arrange the smaller pieces of bread in the middle of four soup or pasta bowls, dividing them evenly among the bowls. Place the red snapper fillets right on top of the bread, then divide the clams and mussels among the bowls, arranging them around the fish. Place the shrimp and octopus on top or around the fish, then add broth to cover the fish, about 1 cup (240 ml) per serving. Finish by placing the larger piece of bread on a diagonal over the side of the bowl. Serve immediately.

LUCA'S TIPS: This recipe takes a little organization, as it includes four different kinds of seafood cooked separately and all put together into the same dish at the end. If you organize your time efficiently, while the octopus is cooking you can make just about everything else—the shrimp, clams and mussels, and toasted bread, cooked one at a time in the same pan, rinsing the pan out between ingredients.

Use the Flip It and Kiss It technique from page 142 when cooking the red snapper fillets.

You could add chunks of potatoes to this dish, as they do in the south of Italy.

HERB-CRUSTED BAKED MONKFISH WITH EGGPLANT CAPONATA

Coda di Rospo con Caponata di Melanzane

Monkfish, called the "poor man's lobster" because of the resemblance of its flesh to the fancy crustacean and its low price tag, is one of my favorite types of fish. The Italian name—*coda di rospo*—means "toad's tail"; in some areas they call it "swimming frog." At the fish market, they'll sell the whole fish without the head because the head is extremely big and heavy. If monkfish isn't available, any thick, white-fleshed fish fillet can be used. The *caponata* is one of those dishes that tastes even better the next day, so feel free to make it in advance. This is a great dish for summer.

Serves 4

Preheat the oven to 375°F (190°C).

Combine the butter, parsley, bread crumbs, lemon zest, and salt and pepper, to taste, in a food processor and process for a minute or so until the butter is smooth and the ingredients are fully combined.

Season the fish with salt and pepper on both sides, then spread the bread crumb mixture on top of each fillet, making a ½-inch-thick (12-mm) crust. Remember, the crust is what will make this fish super-delicious, so don't worry if it looks like there's too much. Just be sure you make an even layer. Refrigerate the fish while you work on the caponata (refrigerating ensures that the butter firms up and that when it goes into the oven it will melt slowly to form the crust).

Line a baking sheet with paper towels. Peel the eggplant and cut it into ½-inch (12-mm) cubes. Place them on the prepared baking sheet and sprinkle heavily with salt to get the moisture out (a process called degorging). Place a layer of paper towels over the eggplant and let stand for 30 minutes. Pat the eggplant with paper towels to absorb the liquid that was released.

(continued)

10 tablespoons (140 g) unsalted butter, cut into chunks

1 cup (40 g) chopped fresh parsley

1½ cups (180 g) fine bread crumbs

3 tablespoons finely grated lemon zest

Salt and freshly ground black pepper

4 (6-ounce/170-g) skin-on monkfish fillets

1 (1-pound/455-g) Italian eggplant

3 tablespoons extra-virgin olive oil

½ cup (80 g) capers in brine, rinsed

1 cup (180 g) pitted black olives

1 cup (150 g) cherry tomatoes, halved

1 cup (125 g) pearl onions, peeled and halved,

1 (14.5-ounce/415-g) can chopped San Marzano tomatoes (with juice)

¼ cup (60 ml) apple-cider vinegar

3 tablespoons sugar

1 cup (40 g) fresh basil leaves, julienned

½ cup (120 ml) white wine

Heat 2 tablespoons of the oil in a large sauté pan over medium heat. Add the eggplant in an even layer and season with pepper. Cook, without stirring, for about 2 minutes, then check if they are starting to brown. When they are good to go, turn them all. (We are lightly pan-frying the eggplant to crisp it a little so it won't turn to mush when we cook it with the rest of the ingredients.) Cook the eggplant for about 10 minutes more, turning occasionally, until nicely browned.

Add the capers, olives, cherry tomatoes, and pearl onions and cook for about 10 minutes more, until the onions start to soften. Add the chopped tomatoes (with juice) and ½ cup (120 ml) of water and cook for about 10 minutes, until the mixture has thickened, then add the vinegar and sugar and cook for 5 minutes to combine the flavors. Remove from the heat and add the basil. Set aside.

Remove the fish from the refrigerator; the crust should be hardened. In a large ovenproof sauté pan, heat the remaining 1 tablespoon oil over medium-high heat until screaming hot. Place the fish in the pan with the crust side facing up (you'll cook them just on one side; no flipping). As the fish cooks, the fillets will shrink, and the crust will be bigger than the fish. Not to worry! When you transfer the pan to the oven, the crust will kind of hug the fillets as they cook. Sear for about 5 minutes, until a nice crust is formed on the bottom and the fish can move in the pan. If you're not using a nonstick pan, they may need a little help from a spatula. Remove from the heat, add the wine, and transfer to the oven. Bake for 10 to 12 minutes, until cooked through.

Heat the caponata until just warmed through. Divide the fish among four serving plates and serve the caponata alongside.

BRANZINO WITH HEIRLOOM CHERRY TOMATOES, FAVA BEAN AND MINT PUREE, AND ASPARAGUS SAUCE

Branzino con Pomodorini, Purea di Fava e Menta con Salsa di Asparagi

FOR THE FISH

4 (1- to 2-pound/455- to 910-g) branzini, filleted

Coarse sea salt

1 lemon, thinly sliced, seeds removed

2 garlic cloves, roughly chopped

Leaves from 1 fresh thyme sprig

FOR THE PUREE

Salt

1 pound yellow fava beans in the shell, soaked in water to cover overnight and drained, or 8 ounces frozen shelled fava beans (about 1½ cups/225 g)

1 tablespoon extra-virgin olive oil

2 shallots, chopped

3 garlic cloves, chopped

About ½ cup (120 ml) vegetable stock, homemade (page 72) or good-quality store-bought

½ cup (20 g) fresh mint leaves, chopped

Freshly ground black pepper

While this restaurant-style *secondo* includes four separate components, each is relatively easy to put together and can be prepared in advance and finished in minutes. Branzino, also known as Mediterranean sea bass, is a moist, white-fleshed fish with skin that crisps up nicely as it hits a searing-hot pan. If unavailable in your area, black sea bass, red snapper, or trout may be substituted. If you are on a budget, you can use just two branzini and serve one fillet per dish, enough to satisfy most appetites. Ask your butcher to fillet the fish for you and to wrap the bones, heads, and tails separately so you can use them to make fish stock (see the recipe on page 65).

I like to use a variety of colors of heirloom cherry tomatoes for this dish, but of course you can also use standard red cherry tomatoes. If you use fresh fava beans, you will need to soak them in water overnight and then shell them. If you can find frozen favas, you'll save yourself some time.

Serves 4

FIRST, WE'LL PREP THE FISH:
Score the fish a few times with a knife and sprinkle the flesh with some salt. Arrange the lemon slices, garlic, and thyme over one fillet from each pair. Find the matching fillet and place it on top, as if you were reconstructing the fish. Wrap each tightly in plastic wrap and refrigerate for at least 8 hours, or overnight.

THEN WE'LL MAKE THE PUREE:
Fill a large bowl with ice and water to make an ice bath. Bring a large pot of salted water to a boil. If you are using fresh fava beans, shell the fava beans by pulling the stem string down the length of each pod to release the bean, as you would shell a pea pod. Discard the outer pod. Place the shelled fava beans in the boiling water and cook for about 5 minutes to loosen the waxy outer skin and soften them a little. Using

a slotted spoon, transfer the beans to the ice bath and let cool for a minute, then peel off the thick, waxy outer covering from each of the beans. For frozen beans, simply blanch them in the boiling water for 2 minutes, then, using a slotted spoon, transfer the beans to the ice bath to cool. Bring the blanching water back to a boil.

Meanwhile, in a medium sauté pan, heat the oil over medium heat. Add the shallots and garlic and cook for about 3 minutes, until softened. Add the blanched beans and cook for 2 to 3 minutes to combine the flavors. Transfer to a food processor, and with the machine running, slowly add enough vegetable stock through the feed tube to process into a chunky puree. Add the mint and process to incorporate it. Return the puree to the pan and season with salt and pepper; keep warm.

PREP AND MARINATE THE CHERRY TOMATOES:
Add some more ice to your ice bath, if necessary. Using a paring knife, score a tiny "X" on the bottom of each cherry tomato. Add the cherry tomatoes to the boiling blanching water and cook for about 15 seconds to loosen the tomato skins. Using a slotted spoon, transfer the tomatoes to the ice bath. Let cool for about 15 seconds, then transfer the cherry tomatoes to a medium bowl and peel them.

Toss the peeled tomatoes with the basil, oil, and vinegar. Season with salt and pepper. Set aside to marinate while you finish the dish.

NOW WE'LL MAKE THE SAUCE:
Drain the water in which you blanched the cherry tomatoes, fill the pot with fresh water, salt it, and bring it to a boil. Set up a fresh ice bath. Add the asparagus and cook for about 5 minutes, until slightly softened and bright green in color. Using a slotted spoon, transfer the asparagus to the ice bath. Reserve 1 cup (240 ml) of the cooking water. Let the asparagus cool for a minute, then remove the asparagus and chop it roughly. Place it in a food processor or blender along with the shallot and reserved 1 cup (240 ml) of cooking water. Process until smooth. Strain through a fine-mesh strainer into a medium saucepan, pressing on the solids with the back of a spoon to extract all the liquid. Discard any solids left in the strainer. Set the pan over medium-high heat, bring to a boil, and cook for about 10 minutes, until reduced to a medium-thick sauce. Stir in the butter one piece at a time until melted and incorporated. Season with salt and pepper and remove from the heat. Keep warm.

(continued)

FOR THE MARINATED CHERRY TOMATOES

2 cups (300 g) red and/or yellow heirloom cherry tomatoes

½ cup (20 g) loosely packed basil leaves, chopped

1 tablespoon extra-virgin olive oil

1 tablespoon red-wine vinegar

Salt and freshly ground black pepper

FOR THE SAUCE

40 asparagus spears, woody ends trimmed (see Note)

1 shallot

2 tablespoons unsalted butter, cut into 4 chunks

Salt and freshly ground black pepper

TO SERVE

4 tablespoons (60 ml) extra-virgin olive oil

Microgreens

NOTE: Save the woody asparagus ends for making stock for the Asparagus and Lemon Risotto on page 82.

NOW IT'S TIME TO COOK THE FISH AND SERVE THE DISH:

Take the fish out of the refrigerator and remove the plastic wrap. Separate the fillets and remove the lemons. Heat 2 tablespoons of the oil in a large sauté pan over medium-high heat until screaming hot. Add four fish fillets to the pan, skin-side down, pressing a few times on the fillets with a spatula during the first 30 seconds of cooking to prevent the fish from curling. Cook until 90 percent cooked through, 3 to 5 minutes. Quickly flip the fish and cook for about 20 seconds more, until the fish is just cooked through. Carefully transfer the fillets to a plate. Repeat with the remaining 2 tablespoons oil and remaining four fish fillets.

Spoon the asparagus sauce into the center of each of four plates. Stir the mint into the bean puree and spoon it over the asparagus sauce. Place a few tomatoes on top of the puree, arranged so they act as a stand for the fish. Plate two fillets per serving, placing the fillets one on top of the other at a slight angle to give the dish that cool, restaurant-style presentation. Finish with a pinch of microgreens.

Flip It and Kiss It

Kiss is a term we use in the culinary world: It means to let the food touch the hot pan for a few seconds, as fast as a quick kiss. First, we cook the fish, skin-side down, until it is cooked about 90 percent of the way through; as it cooks, the skin crisps up, and you see a white line of doneness rise up the fillet. When the white line reaches that 90 percent mark, we flip the fish and kiss the flesh side to the pan for just a few seconds to finish cooking. I learned this from watching YouTube videos of Chef Gordon Ramsay demonstrating the technique.

HALIBUT WITH WHITE ASPARAGUS RISOTTO

Ippoglosso con Risotto Agli Asparagi Bianchi

FOR THE PUREE

Salt

8 ounces (225 g) fresh or frozen sweet peas

1 tablespoon extra-virgin olive oil

Freshly ground black pepper

1 tablespoon fresh lemon juice

FOR THE RISOTTO

Salt

½ bunch (about 7 ounces/ 200 g) white asparagus, trimmed

2 cups (480 ml) vegetable stock, homemade (page 72) or good-quality store-bought

4 tablespoons (56 g) unsalted butter, at room temperature

1 tablespoon extra-virgin olive oil

½ large shallot, very finely chopped

½ cup (100 g) Arborio rice

½ cup (120 ml) white wine

½ cup (50 g) freshly grated Grana Padano, at room temperature

2 tablespoons chopped fresh parsley

Freshly ground black pepper

If you watch *MasterChef*, I'm sure you'll remember this dish. It was the family mystery box, where the contestants' loved ones made a surprise visit. Many people said that challenge was the moment of no return for me. At that point in the season, I had made one good dish, some dishes in the middle, and some dishes at the bottom. But everything changed when I made this halibut. I was back in the running.

The challenge was to create a dish inspired by the people we love: something that had meaning for them, maybe something that we had cooked for them in the past and that showed them what we had learned so far in the competition. That day, we were down to just seven people, and of course everyone wanted to shine.

As I mentioned before, the first thing I ever cooked for my wife, Cate, was my Asparagus and Lemon Risotto (page 82). Cate loves whitefish, so I decided to combine the two to create a restaurant-quality dish. It was also a way to try to redeem myself after the catastrophic crab risotto I'd made a few weeks before; I needed to show the judges and all of America that I could really cook risotto—and Italian food in general!

White asparagus has a very short season, in early spring, so that's the time to make this recipe. For the fish, I used halibut, but you can use any white-fleshed fish; even monkfish would work nicely. I wrapped the fish in caul fat for that extra bit of flavor. Your butcher should have some caul fat; it is usually sold frozen in bulk. You may not use all of it, but it's a good thing to have in the freezer, and it is very cheap. The sweet-pea puree is more of a garnish than a side; it's there to give some color and brighten up the flavor.

Serves 4

FIRST, WE'LL TAKE CARE OF THE PUREE:

Fill a large bowl with ice and water to make an ice bath. Bring a large pot of salted water to a boil. Add the peas and cook for 2 to 3 minutes, until they turn bright green. Using a slotted spoon, transfer the peas to the ice bath. Let cool for a minute, then, using a slotted spoon, transfer the peas to a blender. Add ¼ cup (60 ml) water and the oil and blend until smooth. Pass the puree through a fine-mesh strainer into a small bowl, pressing on the solids with the back of a spoon; discard the solids left in the strainer. Season the puree with salt and pepper and add the lemon juice. It will taste very acidic now, but that's OK, because when you eat it with the rest of the dish, everything will balance out. Spoon the puree into a squeeze bottle and set aside.

Preheat the oven to 375°F (190°C).

TO MAKE THE RISOTTO:

Fill a large bowl with ice and water to make an ice bath. Bring a large pot of salted water to a boil. Add the asparagus and cook for about 3 minutes, until slightly softened. Using a slotted spoon, transfer the asparagus to the prepared ice bath. Let cool for a minute, then remove the asparagus and pat it dry with a paper towel. Chop the asparagus into ½-inch (12-mm) pieces.

In a medium saucepan, bring the stock to a simmer. Keep it at a low simmer while you make the risotto.

Melt 1 tablespoon of the butter in the oil in a medium saucepan over medium heat. Add the shallots and rice and toast the rice, stirring, for about 3 minutes, until the rice starts looking chalky. Add the wine, raise the heat to medium-high, and cook, stirring constantly, until the wine has been absorbed, about 3 minutes. Reduce the heat to medium.

We'll begin to add our stock now, and at the same time test our multitasking skills by cooking the halibut in between additions (see below). Keep stirring and adding the hot stock 1 cup (240 ml) at a time, as the rice asks for it, waiting until the previous addition has been absorbed before adding the next. At the 10-minute mark, add 1 tablespoon of the remaining butter and the asparagus, reserving a few tips for garnish. Keep on stirring to bring the starch out of the rice and get your risotto very creamy. At the 17-minute mark, taste the rice. It should still be too al dente, but we are getting closer. Keep cooking, adding stock as needed in ½-cup (120-ml) increments, until the rice is just tender and creamy-looking but still al dente. The total cooking time will be about 18 minutes. Remove from the heat and add the remaining 2 tablespoons butter (cut it into cubes first), the cheese, and the parsley. Stir vigorously, adding a little more stock if it is looking too thick. When the butter has all melted, the risotto is ready. Season with salt and pepper.

(continued)

FOR THE HALIBUT

4 (6-ounce/170-g) skinless halibut fillets, each 2 inches (5 cm) thick

Salt and freshly ground black pepper

8 ounces (225 g) caul fat, soaked in salted cold water for 30 minutes and drained

2 tablespoons extra-virgin olive oil

WHILE THE RISOTTO COOKS, MAKE THE HALIBUT:

Season the fish with salt and pepper. Lay the caul fat on a work surface, spreading it to form a large thin sheet, and pat it dry with a paper towel. Cut out squares large enough to wrap each piece of fish completely, then wrap the fish, tucking the ends under to form a package.

Heat the oil in a large ovenproof nonstick pan until screaming hot. Add the fish and cook for 30 seconds, then reduce the heat to medium so the fat can gently melt into the fish. Cook until golden brown, 3 to 4 minutes, then flip the fish and cook for about 4 minutes more, until golden brown on the second side. Place the fish in the oven and bake for about 5 minutes, until just cooked through.

TO SERVE:

Spoon the risotto onto four round plates, lay a fish fillet on each, and, like an artist giving the final touches to his masterpiece, squeeze the puree all around the plate in a circular motion. Garnish each plate with a few of the reserved asparagus tips.

LUCA'S TIPS: It is important to not overlap the caul fat when you wrap the fish, or the bottom layer will not cook. If, by the time the fish is cooked, some parts of the fat didn't melt, take them off before serving, following my rule that "if it is not edible, it should not go on a plate."

Use white asparagus as much as you can when it is in season in early spring. It is sweet and delicious and so good for you. One of my favorite ways to eat white asparagus is simply blanched in boiling water, served with a fried egg on top, and finished with some shaved pecorino and cracked black pepper.

Checking Your Fish with a Skewer

The secret to making sure that oven-baked fish is cooked through: Take it out of the oven, poke it with a metal skewer right through the middle, and hold the skewer there for 15 seconds. Pull it out and touch the skewer: If the skewer feels just warm, the fish is perfectly cooked. If it's cold, put the fish back into the oven. If it's super-hot, well . . . tough luck. It will be better next time!

VENETIAN-STYLE CALF'S LIVER

Fegato alla Veneziana

If you followed *MasterChef* Season 3, you know that this is the dish that sent me home after the first round. Looking back, I realize that making this was a bold move but wasn't the best strategy. I wanted to cook something that really showed who I am and where I come from. Joe Bastianich liked it because he is very familiar with the dish, but Chef Gordon Ramsay and Chef Graham Elliot probably had never had it before, and, at the end, it was poorly executed, with the liver a little overcooked and the polenta not as smooth as I wanted it to be. When I was eliminated, I was devastated. At that moment, I never would have guessed that one year later I was going to be here writing my very first book.

This is a dish that my dad would make for me at home once in a while, and its history takes us back to Roman times, when it was cooked with figs. Figs were too expensive for average people, so they started using more affordable white onions instead. The original recipe calls for sage, and you can add a little at the end if you like. I am sure many grandmothers back in Italy cooked the liver all the way through, but I like to keep mine medium-rare. Serve it with polenta (page 172), either cooked with cream and cheese and served straight from the pan or cooked with water, firmed up, and grilled. Mashed potatoes is another good option.

2 tablespoons extra-virgin olive oil

2 white onions, thinly sliced

Salt and freshly ground black pepper

1 cup (240 ml) vegetable stock, homemade (page 72) or good-quality store-bought

1½ pounds (680 g) calf's liver, cleaned of excess sinew or silver skin

All-purpose flour

¾ cup (180 ml) white wine

2 tablespoons chopped fresh parsley

Serves 4

In a medium sauté pan, heat 1 tablespoon of the oil over medium heat. Add the onions, season with salt and pepper, and sauté until they start to soften, about 5 minutes. Add the stock, bring it to a simmer, and cook until the onions are very soft and the stock has been absorbed, about 20 minutes. Remove from the heat and set aside.

Pat the liver dry with paper towels and cut it into 2-inch (5-cm) strips. Season the liver with salt and pepper and lightly dust with some flour. This will give a little crust to the meat.

In a large sauté pan, heat the remaining 1 tablespoon of oil over medium-high heat until screaming hot, almost smoking. Add the liver and sear for about 3 minutes, until deeply browned on the underside but still pink in the center. Turn the liver pieces, add the onions to the pan, then

(continued)

immediately add the wine and sprinkle in about 1 teaspoon of flour to help thicken the sauce. Cook for about 2 minutes more, until the liver is just cooked through and the sauce has thickened. Add the parsley. Taste the sauce and adjust the salt and pepper, if needed. Divide the liver and onions, including the sauce, among four plates and serve immediately.

LUCA'S TIPS: To make slicing your liver easier, first freeze it for about 45 minutes to firm up. Even easier, have your butcher do it for you when he cleans the liver, or buy packaged presliced liver.

The liver should be served medium-rare to medium, so it is very important to get the pan very hot before you start to cook it, and then add the wine right away after you turn it.

THE VIETNAMESE SOUP CHALLENGE

I was petrified. We had to recreate a braised pork noodle soup that Chef Ramsay ate years ago in Vietnam. I wound up cooking the best dish of the evening, and at that point became unstoppable.

PANCETTA-WRAPPED VEAL CUTLET WITH RADICCHIO, APPLES, AND WHITE-WINE SAUCE

Scaloppine di Vitello Avvolte in Pancetta con Radicchio e Mele e Salsa al Vino Bianco

FOR THE VEAL

8 veal cutlets (about 1 pound/455 g total), thinly pounded scaloppini-style to about 7 inches (17 cm) long

Leaves from 1 bunch fresh sage

1 cup (100 g) thinly shaved Grana Padano (shaved with a vegetable peeler)

32 very thin slices pancetta (about 1 pound/455 g)

FOR THE RADICCHIO

2 tablespoons extra-virgin olive oil, plus more for drizzling

1 white onion, very thinly sliced

1 head radicchio, halved, cored, and very thinly sliced

1 small Belgian endive, halved lengthwise, then very thinly sliced crosswise

Salt and freshly ground black pepper

1 large red apple

1 cup (240 ml) white wine

1 cup (240 ml) chicken stock, homemade (page 73) or good-quality store-bought

This is another *MasterChef* dish that made history. We were down to the top 3—Jessie, Natasha, and me—and headed to our last elimination challenge. Jessie had won the last Mystery Box, so she got first pick on the protein she'd be cooking. She had to choose between Alaskan King crab, Japanese Kobe beef, and Italian Grana Padano cheese. I almost had a heart attack when I saw the crab, because everybody knew how much I don't like to cook with crab. Somehow, and really I don't know how it happened, but those two lovely ladies worked things out so I would be left to cook with the king of Italian cheeses. Are you kidding me? You give cheese to the only Italian in the competition?

I was allowed to choose from a fridgeful of proteins that would play a supporting role for the recipe, with the cheese remaining the star of the dish. Initially, I thought of a beautiful breast of duck, but when I saw the veal cutlet, I thought it would be smarter if I stuck to my roots. And when we are talking about my roots, of course frico comes up. Frico is made with a lot of cheese (see page 129 for my recipe), so I decided to serve these two classic Friuli dishes together. The judges liked my dish; the only criticism was that the plate lacked color. I completely agreed with them, but I stuck to my roots. This is a very warm, homey, rustic dish, and that's just how it's done back in Friuli.

Serves 4

FIRST, WE'LL ROLL UP OUR VEAL:

Lay the cutlets on a cutting board. Starting 1½ inches (4 cm) from the bottom of each cutlet, arrange 4 or 5 sage leaves over each cutlet, touching but not overlapping, leaving 1½ inches (4 cm) bare at the top of the cutlet. Cover the sage leaves with the cheese. (Of course, in this case, overlapping is allowed. The more cheese, the better!)

Roll up the cutlets, starting at the end closest to you; roll away from you and pull the cutlet toward you slightly as you roll to keep it tight. Secure with a toothpick, if needed. Set them on a plate as you finish rolling each one.

Lay a piece of plastic wrap on the cutting board and lay 4 slices of pancetta over it, two next to each other overlapping just a little bit and the other 2 underneath, overlapping again a little. So now you should have more or less a rectangle of pancetta on the wrap. Take the toothpicks out of the veal rolls if you used them. Place one of the rolled cutlets at the edge of the pancetta, seam-side down, starting from the edge. Roll the wrap on it away from you, squeezing it tightly, and when you get to the point that if you were to keep rolling the wrap would get wrapped into the meat, stop and very slowly pull the wrap away from the pancetta so the pancetta will stick to the meat. Then keep on rolling until the pancetta is completely wrapped around the cutlet. I am telling you, it really sounds harder than it actually is! Repeat for the remaining cutlets using the same sheet of plastic, place them on a plate, and put it in the refrigerator while you continue with your recipe.

NOW WE COME TO THE RADICCHIO:

In a large sauté pan, heat the oil over medium heat. Add the onions and cook for about 5 minutes, until softened. If the pan gets too dry, add a little water to help soften the onions. Add the radicchio and endive, season with salt and pepper, and drizzle a little oil on top. Cook for about 5 minutes to release the water from the vegetables. Grate the apple on the large holes of a box grater directly into the pan (so you don't lose the juice—if this is daunting, grate the apple over a plate and add the grated flesh and the juices to the pan all at once). Cook, stirring often, for about 5 minutes, until the pan starts to get dry. Add the wine, bring to a simmer, and cook until the wine has been almost completely absorbed, about 10 minutes. Add the stock, return to a simmer, and cook for 10 minutes more, or until the liquid has been absorbed and the vegetables are very soft. Taste and season with more salt and pepper, if needed.

Preheat the oven to 425°F (220°C).

TIME TO WORK THE SAUCE:

In a small shallow saucepan, heat the oil over medium heat. Add the garlic, shallots, rosemary, and thyme and cook for 3 to 4 minutes, until aromatic, then add the wine and cook until it has reduced by half, 3 to 4 minutes. Add the stock and cook until it has reduced by half, about 5 minutes more. Strain the sauce through a fine-mesh strainer into a clean saucepan; discard the solids left in the strainer. Bring the sauce to a simmer over medium heat, then reduce the heat to very low, add the butter, and stir to melt it. Cook for 5 minutes to thicken the sauce a little and season with salt and pepper. Add the lemon juice. Keep warm.

(continued on page 154)

FOR THE SAUCE

1 tablespoon extra-virgin olive oil

2 garlic cloves, peeled and smashed

1 small shallot, halved

1 sprig fresh rosemary

3 sprigs fresh thyme

½ cup (120 ml) white wine

½ cup (120 ml) chicken stock, homemade (page 73) or good-quality store-bought

2 tablespoons unsalted butter

Salt and freshly ground black pepper

2 tablespoons fresh lemon juice

MY FREE PASS TO THE *MASTERCHEF* FINALE

Veal, Grana Padano, and radicchio: There's nothing more Italian than these three ingredients, and this was the first time in the competition that I actually succeeded in making an Italian dish.

AND NOW TO COOK THE VEAL:

Heat a large ovenproof sauté pan over medium-high heat until screaming hot. Drizzle in just a little bit of oil (you don't need that much because the pancetta will release a lot of fat as it cooks). Add the veal and sear for 60 to 90 seconds, until it is browned and crisp and the fat starts rendering from the pancetta. Turn the veal and reduce the heat to medium to avoid burning the pancetta. Sear the veal on all sides, 60 to 90 seconds per side, until nicely browned and crisp all over. Transfer the pan to the oven and bake for 2 to 3 minutes, until the veal is medium-rare, with the outside layers cooked through and the inside nice and pink. Remove from the oven and let rest for 3 minutes, then cut the veal rolls into ½- to 1-inch (1.25- to 2.5-cm) slices.

TO SERVE:

I like to use rectangular plates and set the radicchio mixture on the four plates as a bed for the veal, but you can use any shape plate you like. Arrange the sliced veal rolls on top, spooning a little sauce over the top, and serve.

LUCA'S TIPS: It is super-important you get those Grana Padano shavings as thin as possible, because you want them to melt as the veal is cooked.

Here in the States you can find radicchio almost all year long, but the real radicchio di Treviso comes into season in the fall around the end of October, beginning of November. It's shaped like an endive and red, and it's a favorite of mine. It makes me think of home, as Treviso is just thirty minutes from where I grew up. If you do find real radicchio di Treviso, halve it, core it, wrap it in pancetta, and grill it. You won't believe how good it is this way.

COTECHINO WITH SAUERKRAUT

Muset e Brovade

No Christmas season in Friuli passed without eating *cotechino con brovade*, and whenever I'm home in the winter, I'm sure to ask my mom to make this special dish for me.

I am sorry, readers, but I'll be direct and to the point to describe what *cotechino* is: It's every part of the pig that is not used for prosciutto, salame, *porchetta*, or whatever else, ground together with a lot of fat and made into sausage. Where I am from we use a lot of *musetto*, from the Italian word *muso,* which means "face" or "snout" (again, pardon me for the directness!). You will find cotechino in very traditional Italian grocery stores during the holiday season. Most will be imported from Italy, though my friends from Sorriso Italian Salumeria in Astoria, Queens, make a delicious homemade cotechino. If you cannot find cotechino, you could try *zampone*, which is the leg of the pig from the heel to the knee, and cook it the same way.

In the rest of Italy, this dish is served with lentils for good luck. In Friuli, it is served with *brovade*, cabbage that's been marinated in grape pomace (a by-product of winemaking), probably because we don't believe in luck, just hard work. Brovade is deep red in color and has tons of acidity; my grandmothers would add some apple to cut the acidity. Traditional brovade is almost impossible to find, even here in New York City, so in this recipe, I add some apple-cider vinegar to plain sauerkraut to give it a little extra acidity. I like to serve this with salsa verde on the side; it's not traditional, but I have noticed that people who are not very familiar with this dish like it better that way.

Serves 4 to 6

PREPARE THE COTECHINO:

Using a fork, pierce some holes into the cotechino casings. Place them in a large saucepan with enough cold water to cover them by a few inches. Set the pan over high heat and bring the water to a boil. Reduce the heat a little to maintain a slow boil and cook for 2 hours. Drain the cotechino and set aside.

(continued)

FOR THE COTECHINO

2 (1-pound/455-g) cotechino sausages

FOR THE SAUERKRAUT

2 teaspoons extra-virgin olive oil

1 cup finely chopped bacon (5 ounces/140 g)

4 garlic cloves, peeled and smashed

2 white onions, finely chopped

2 pounds (910 g) prepared sauerkraut (with juice) (about 3 cups)

¼ cup (60 ml) apple-cider vinegar

1 large red apple, peeled

2 cups (480 ml) chicken stock, homemade (page 73) or good-quality store-bought

5 fresh sage leaves

4 bay leaves

4 whole cloves

1 tablespoon paprika

1 teaspoon freshly grated nutmeg

1 teaspoon ground cinnamon

Freshly ground black pepper

(continued)

FOR THE SALSA VERDE

2 cups (80 g) fresh parsley leaves

2 hard-boiled egg yolks

1 slice day-old bread, crust removed, bread torn into pieces

2 garlic cloves

1 tablespoon drained and rinsed capers

2 tablespoons white-wine vinegar

Salt and freshly ground black pepper

Extra-virgin olive oil

MAKE THE SAUERKRAUT:

Heat the oil in a large saucepan over medium heat. Add the bacon and garlic and cook until the bacon releases its fat and starts to crisp, about 5 minutes. Add the onions and cook until softened, about 5 minutes. Add the sauerkraut (with juice) and the vinegar, raise the heat to medium-high, and cook until most of the juices have been absorbed, about 10 minutes.

Coarsely grate the apple on the large holes of a box grater directly into the pan. Add 1 cup (240 ml) of the stock, the sage leaves, bay leaves, cloves, paprika, nutmeg, and cinnamon and season with pepper. Bring to a simmer and cook until the stock is absorbed, about 20 minutes. Add the remaining 1 cup (240 ml) of stock, reduce the heat to low, and cook, stirring occasionally, for at least 30 minutes more (the more you cook it, the better!), until most of the liquid has been absorbed and the sauerkraut has a nice, saucy coating.

MEANWHILE, MAKE THE SALSA VERDE:

In a food processor, combine the parsley, egg yolks, bread, garlic, capers, vinegar, and salt and pepper and process. Through the feed tube or hole in the top of the machine, add enough oil until the mixture has the consistency of pesto. Transfer the sauce to a serving bowl.

TO SERVE:

Spread the sauerkraut on a serving platter. Slice the cotechino and arrange the slices on top. Pass the salsa verde at the table for guests to take as they like.

LUCA'S TIPS: If you let the sauerkraut you've prepared rest for at least half a day in its juices, it will taste even better, making this a great make-ahead recipe.

You can cook the sauerkraut for even longer than I've suggested; cook it a couple of hours and it will be very good. Cook it for six hours and it will be great. (You will probably need to add some liquid so it doesn't dry out.) The next day, forget about it—the best!

If you want to stay very traditional and care more about flavor than presentation, slice the cotechino after you boil it, add it to the cooked sauerkraut, and warm it all together for 30 minutes before serving. That is what my nonna Anita and my mother used to do. Again, if you keep it on low heat for hours and hours, you will be very happy. When you taste it, you will think you have died and gone to heaven.

MY MOTHER'S MEATBALLS

Le Polpette della Mamma

1 ciabatta roll, cut into small cubes

About 1 cup (240 ml) milk

1 pound (455 g) ground beef

½ cup (50 g) freshly grated Grana Padano

½ cup (30 g) minced white onion

4 teaspoons minced garlic

2 tablespoons white wine

1 large egg

2 large egg yolks

⅓ cup (13 g) finely chopped fresh parsley

1½ teaspoons freshly grated lemon zest

2 teaspoons salt

1 teaspoon freshly ground black pepper

¼ cup (60 ml) extra-virgin olive oil

3 or 4 sprigs fresh rosemary

This is another recipe that takes me back to when I was growing up in Italy. I can't even imagine how many times I ate these meatballs when I was a kid—and even as a grown-up kid grabbing them cold from the fridge at six in the morning after a night out clubbing. The translation for *polpette* is "meatballs," but my mother's were bigger than meatballs, smaller than hamburgers, not quite flat and not quite round. All the garlic, the freshness of the lemon, and the moisture of the bread dipped in milk makes this meatball the best I've ever tasted. You can serve them with anything you like—salad, roasted potatoes (page 171), grilled vegetables (page 174), or polenta (page 172).

Makes 8 large meatballs

Place the bread in a medium bowl and add enough of the milk to cover it. Set aside to soak for about 30 minutes, until completely soggy.

In a large bowl, combine the beef, cheese, onions, garlic, wine, egg, egg yolks, parsley, lemon zest, salt and pepper. Stir well with a wooden spoon, or put on disposable gloves and mix everything together with your hands.

Squeeze the bread to release most of the milk. Add the bread to the bowl with the beef mixture and mix well.

Take a generous amount of the meat mixture (about 4 ounces, or 115 g), put it on the palm of your hand, squeeze it a little to round the edges, and then press it with the other hand to flatten it a little. Repeat with the remaining meat mixture, setting the formed meatballs on a plate until ready to cook.

Heat the oil in very large sauté pan over medium-high heat until screaming hot. Add the rosemary sprigs, then add the meatballs. Cook, without turning, for 3 minutes to give them a nice crust. (If you turn them in the first 3 minutes, they'll fall apart.) Turn the meatballs and cook for 3 minutes more, basting them with the juices being released from the meat. Reduce the heat to low, cover the pan, and cook for 8 to 10 minutes, until cooked through, basting them frequently. Transfer to a platter and serve family-style.

COOKING UNDER PRESSURE

I knew I had a great dish in my hands, but it was all down to the pressure cooker.

When the moment of truth came and I opened the lid, the short ribs (recipe on page 164) were my ticket to victory.

RACK OF LAMB WITH POTATO PUREE

Carre di Agnello con Puree di Patate

FOR THE POTATO PUREE

1 pound (455 g) Yukon Gold potatoes, peeled and cut into small cubes

1½ cups (360 ml) whole milk

½ cup (120 ml) heavy cream

Salt and freshly ground white or black pepper

½ cup (115 g) sour cream

2 tablespoons chopped fresh chives

FOR THE LAMB

1 (1½- to 2-pound/680- to 910-g) rack of lamb

Salt and freshly ground black pepper

2 tablespoons extra-virgin olive oil

3 garlic cloves

2 sprigs fresh rosemary

2 sprigs fresh thyme

1 cup (240 ml) beef stock, homemade (page 89) or good-quality store-bought

This is a very fancy dish. Anything with a beautiful, just-carved lamb chop is going to be super-special. Ask your butcher for a whole rack of lamb. She will ask you if you want all the fat cut out, and you will say yes, and then you will ask her in a very sweet way if she could French the bones for you, cut the excess meat, and save it for you on the side. Then you can freeze it to later make a lamb ragout the same way you cooked the veal for the chestnut pappardelle on page 112. I serve this with a potato puree that's like mashed potatoes but even smoother and creamier.

Serves 4

FIRST, WE'LL WORK ON THE POTATOES:
Place the potatoes in a medium saucepan and cover them with the milk and cream. Season with salt and pepper. Set the pan over medium heat, cover, and bring just to a boil. Reduce the heat to maintain a simmer and cook for 20 minutes, or until the potatoes are softened. Strain the potatoes through a fine-mesh strainer set over a medium bowl, reserving the liquid. Pass the potatoes through a food mill into a large bowl, or place them in a large bowl and coarsely mash them by hand with a potato masher to a rough mashed-potato consistency. Add the sour cream and chives; add a little of the reserved liquid if the potatoes are too thick. Set aside.

Preheat the oven to 450°F (230°C).

NOW LET'S ATTACK THE LAMB:
Season the lamb heavily with salt and pepper. In a large heavy-bottomed ovenproof sauté pan, heat the oil over medium heat. Add the garlic, rosemary, and thyme and cook for 2 to 3 minutes, until aromatic. Then crank up the heat, and when the pan is screaming hot, place the rack of lamb, fat-side down, in the pan. Cook for 4 to 5 minutes to render the fat and get a nice sear on the lamb, then turn the rack and sear for 3 to 4 more minutes on the second side. Add the stock, let it sizzle for a minute, then place the pan in the oven and roast until a meat thermometer inserted in the center of the meat reads between 125° and 130°F (52° to 55°C) for rare to medium-rare, 20 to 25 minutes (check it at 20 minutes), or 135° to 140°F (57° to 60°C) for medium-rare to medium, 25 to 30 minutes. Remove from the oven and let the lamb rest for 7 to 8 minutes.

WHILE THE LAMB IS IN THE OVEN, WE'LL WORK ON THE SPINACH:

Heat the garlic in the oil in a large sauté pan over medium-high heat until screaming hot. Add the spinach, season with salt and pepper and add the red pepper flakes, if using. Cover, and cook for about 2 minutes, shaking the pan a bit, until the spinach is wilted. Remove from the heat.

FINALLY, WE'LL MAKE THE SAUCE:

In a medium saucepan, heat the oil with the garlic, shallots, rosemary, and thyme over medium-high heat. Add a pinch of salt and pepper and cook for about 5 minutes, until the mixture is aromatic and the garlic is starting to brown. Add the wine, raise the heat to medium-high, and cook until it has reduced by half, about 10 minutes. Add the stock and cook until it has reduced to about ½ cup (120 ml), about 20 minutes. Set aside and keep warm until serving.

TO SERVE:

Set a heat-proof bowl over a pot of simmering water to make a bain-marie and spoon the potato puree into the bowl to reheat. Rewarm the sauce over low heat and melt the butter into the sauce. Slice the lamb between the bones into eight chops.

Set out four large plates and spoon the potato puree in the middle. For each serving, set 2 chops next to each other on the plate (try to make them stand; if not, just set them on the plate as prettily as possible), arrange some of the spinach around the lamb, and spoon some of the sauce on top. Serve immediately.

LUCA'S TIPS: You can serve the lamb with any puree. The puree from my beef short ribs, made with turnips and goat cheese (page 164), would be great, but really just about any puree will work. I love purees (did you notice that yet?). Natasha from *MasterChef* was always making fun of me because I would make so many purees on the show. She would tell me: "Luca, even if you don't win, you can write a book—*My 101 Purees*!"

FOR THE SPINACH

4 garlic cloves, peeled and smashed

1 tablespoon extra-virgin olive oil

6 cups (180 g) spinach leaves

Salt and freshly ground black pepper

Pinch of red pepper flakes (optional)

FOR THE SAUCE

1 tablespoon extra-virgin olive oil

2 garlic cloves, peeled and smashed

1 shallot, finely chopped

2 sprigs fresh rosemary

2 sprigs fresh thyme

Salt and freshly ground black pepper

1½ cups (360 ml) red wine

1½ cups (360 ml) beef stock, homemade (page 89) or good-quality store-bought

TO SERVE

2 tablespoons unsalted butter

NEW YORK STRIP STEAK WITH VANILLA SAUCE

Tagliata con Salsa alla Vaniglia

This is a classic all over Italy. It is called *tagliata* because in Italian the word means "cut," and the steak is sliced before plating. It is always served with arugula and Grana Padano. What is not classic is to serve it with a sauce, especially a vanilla sauce. This idea came from my very good friend Max Convertini. Max is not only an old friend; he is also a great chef, who, for a wedding present, cooked for the guests at my wedding reception. Max and I met here in New York City, and we have been friends for long time. I owe him a lot, because in my months of preparation for *MasterChef*, he was the one I would call on for his advice again and again. Thank you for everything, Max: This recipe is for you!

FOR THE SAUCE

3 cups (720 ml) beef stock, homemade (page 89) or good-quality store-bought

1 vanilla bean

1 sprig fresh rosemary

2 sprigs fresh thyme

Salt

FOR THE STEAK

4 (10- to 12-ounce/280- to 340-g) New York strip steaks (about 1½ inches/4 cm thick)

Salt and freshly ground black pepper

2 tablespoons extra-virgin olive oil

4 tablespoons (56 g) unsalted butter, cut into 4 chunks

4 garlic cloves, peeled and smashed

2 sprigs fresh rosemary

2 sprigs fresh thyme

Serves 4

FIRST, WE'LL MAKE THE SAUCE:

Pour the stock into a medium saucepan. Cut the vanilla-bean pod in half lengthwise and scrape out the seeds using a paring knife. Add both the seeds and the pod to the stock, then add the rosemary and thyme. Set the pan over medium-high heat, bring to a boil, and cook for 30 to 40 minutes, until it has reduced to about ⅓ cup (75 ml). Strain through a fine-mesh strainer into a clean saucepan. Taste and season with salt, if needed. Set over low heat to keep warm.

NOW WE'LL COOK THE STEAK:

Season the steaks heavily with salt and pepper and set aside.

Heat two large sauté pans over medium-high heat until screaming hot. Add 1 tablespoon of oil to each. Add the steaks, 2 to a pan, and cook, resisting the urge to touch them, for 4 minutes to create a nice crust, then flip them and add 2 tablespoons butter, 2 garlic cloves, 1 sprig of rosemary, and 1 sprig of thyme to each pan. Use a spoon to baste the steaks with the melting butter. Cook for just 4 minutes, then transfer them to a cutting board and let rest for 4 minutes.

MAKE THE ARUGULA SALAD:

Place the arugula in a medium bowl and add a drizzle of oil and a quick drizzle of vinegar. Season with salt and pepper and toss to coat.

TO SERVE:

Divide the salad among four plates. Thinly slice the steaks against the grain and arrange the slices on top of the salad. Drizzle with some of the sauce and sprinkle with cheese. Serve immediately.

LUCA'S TIPS: I use New York strip steaks, but you can also use sirloin steak; both cuts come from the loin. The New York is from the bottom part and will have less fat than the sirloin, which comes from the top.

You'll need to heat up two sauté pans in which to cook the steaks. Four steaks in the same pan could seriously affect the quality of your sear; the steaks will release a lot of juice into the pan, so if you crowd the pan, you will wind up boiling the meat rather than searing it!

This recipe will produce a medium-rare steak, which, to me, is the only way to eat a steak. As a rule, steaks need to rest for at least half as long as you cook them, so for a great medium-rare, 1½-inch- (4-cm-) thick steak, cook it for 4 minutes on each side and then rest it for 4 minutes before serving.

FOR THE SALAD

1 cup (20 g) arugula

Extra-virgin olive oil

Balsamic vinegar

Salt and freshly ground black pepper

TO SERVE

Shaved Grana Padano

BRAISED BEEF SHORT RIBS WITH CHANTERELLES AND SUNCHOKE PUREE

Brasato di Costolette di Manzo con Galletti e Tobinambur

FOR THE SHORT RIBS

4 (10-ounce/280-g) beef short ribs on the bone

Salt and freshly ground black pepper

2 tablespoons extra-virgin olive oil

2 white onions, finely chopped

2 carrots, finely chopped

2 celery stalks, finely chopped

1 leek, white and light green parts, finely chopped

5 garlic cloves, finely chopped

1 (2-inch/5-cm) piece fresh ginger, peeled and finely chopped

1 jalapeño, seeded and finely chopped (wear plastic gloves when handling)

2 cups (480 ml) balsamic vinegar

1 quart (960 ml) beef stock, homemade (page 89) or good-quality store-bought, plus more if needed

1 (2-ounce/55-g) can anchovies in olive oil, finely chopped

3 tablespoons molasses

2 tablespoons tamarind paste

1 teaspoon whole black peppercorns

2 whole cloves

Ladies and gentlemen, I am so happy to share with you the recipe for my braised beef short ribs, the one I served to Chef Gordon Ramsay, Chef Graham Elliot, and Mr. Joe Bastianich at the *MasterChef* finale. Chef Ramsay said it was a dish he could picture asking for as his last meal.

In Italy, beef short ribs are traditionally cooked in a red-wine braise (like the one we used for the veal with the chestnut pappardelle on page 112) and are served with polenta (see page 172). This recipe is a mix between classic Italian and all that I learned on my *MasterChef* journey. Take the tamarind, for example, an ingredient that is not part of Italian cuisine. I had never even heard of it before I came to the United States, and when I did, it never crossed my mind to use it until I read the Worcestershire sauce label: tamarind, molasses, anchovies, cloves, chiles, and garlic. What a mix of tastes! It made such an impression on me that I based this braise on those very ingredients and went on to win the *MasterChef* title with it.

I am big fan of braised meat. There is something romantic about it. But don't try to braise meat in the middle of summer. You will not find any romance then, and you will be annoyed with me for even suggesting it. Braised meat calls for fall or winter weather, maybe some snow, the house infused with the aroma of spices and you relaxed and sipping wine on the sofa surrounded by loved ones. If you don't have all that time, though, no worries: Braising meat is a low-and-slow cooking technique, so you could do many other useful things while it's cooking.

I paired my short ribs with a sunchoke puree, chanterelle mushrooms, and fresh watercress. Sunchokes, also known as Jerusalem artichokes, are a species of sunflower, in the daisy family, and, unfortunately, are in season just a few months of the year, from fall to early spring. We eat just the root, which looks a lot like ginger and has a nutty taste and crisp texture that turns creamy when cooked. If sunchokes aren't available, you can substitute turnips or parsnips; if you do, I suggest adding a little goat cheese for the creamiest results. On the show, I added fresh black truffles to the sunchoke puree, but they can be very expensive, and you really don't need to go so fancy!

Then there are the chanterelles, my favorite type of mushroom. In Italy we call them *galletti*, which means "rooster," reflecting the top of the mushroom's resemblance to the crest of a rooster. Their season is usually late summer and fall. I had the luxury of the *MasterChef* pantry, so I had immunity to the seasons for this special meal.

I finish the dish with watercress puree brightened with lemon zest and lemon juice. The acidity that this component brings to the dish lightens the flavor, making the dish less heavy. I call this dish "a walk in the forest early morning in the fall": The ribs represent the trees, the puree is the trail where we walk, the mushrooms are everywhere, and the watercress is the wet grass.

Serves 4

FIRST, WE'LL SEAR AND BRAISE THE SHORT RIBS:
Heavily season the short ribs with salt and pepper. Heat the oil in a large saucepan over medium-high heat until screaming hot. Add the ribs and sear them on all sides, about 4 minutes per side, turning them with tongs as you go. It is important to get a nice hard sear so the meat will keep all its natural juices. Transfer the ribs to a roasting pan. Leave any rendered fat in the saucepan.

Add the onions, carrots, celery, leeks, and garlic. Reduce the heat to medium and cook, stirring often, for 5 minutes, or until softened. Add the ginger and jalapeño and cook, stirring, for 1 minute. Put the ribs back in the pan. Add the vinegar, raise the heat to medium-high, and cook for 20 minutes to reduce the vinegar a little. Add enough stock to cover the ribs, then add the anchovies, molasses, tamarind, peppercorns, and cloves. Season with salt and pepper. Bring to a simmer, then reduce the heat to low, cover with foil, and cook for about 3 hours, until the meat is falling-off-the-bone tender. Take the ribs out of the pan, brush off any bits of vegetables from them, and place them in a clean, large pan. Strain the braising liquid through a fine-mesh strainer into the pan. Discard the solids left in the strainer. Keep the pan on the stove over low heat to coat the meat with the delicious juices and form a glaze around it.

(continued)

FOR THE PUREE

1 pound (455 g) sunchokes

1½ cups (360 ml) whole milk

½ cup (120 ml) heavy cream

Salt

½ cup (4 ounces/115 g) soft fresh goat cheese (optional)

Salt and freshly ground black pepper

FOR THE CHANTERELLES

1 tablespoon extra-virgin olive oil

4 garlic cloves, peeled and smashed

5 ounces (140 g) chanterelle mushrooms, cleaned (see page 25)

Salt and freshly ground black pepper

2 sprigs fresh rosemary

2 sprigs fresh thyme

1½ tablespoons unsalted butter

2 tablespoons beef stock, homemade (page 89) or good-quality store-bought

FOR THE GARNISH (OPTIONAL)

1 cup fresh watercress

5 tablespoons (75 ml) extra-virgin olive oil (if making the puree)

1 tablespoon fresh lemon juice (if making the puree)

1 teaspoon freshly grated lemon zest (if making the puree)

WHILE THE MEAT IS BRAISING, WE'LL WORK ON OUR SIDES,
BEGINNING WITH THE SUNCHOKES:

Wash the sunchokes. You can peel them or keep the skin on, as the skin has a lot of flavor. I like my puree to be bright white, so I peel them. The choice is yours. Finely chop the sunchokes; the smaller the pieces, the faster they cook. Combine the milk and cream in a medium saucepan and add the sunchokes. Season with salt. Set over medium heat, bring to a simmer, and simmer until very tender, about 10 minutes. Watch the pan carefully and reduce the heat as needed if the milk and cream threaten to boil over. Strain the sunchokes through a fine-mesh strainer set over a medium bowl, reserving the liquid. Put the sunchokes in a food processor with ¼ cup (60 ml) of the milk and cream mixture and the cheese, if using. Process until you have a super-smooth puree, adding more of the milk and cream mixture, as needed, to achieve the desired consistency. Season with salt and pepper.

NOW WE COME TO THE CHANTERELLES:

In a large sauté pan, heat the oil with the garlic until screaming hot. Add the mushrooms, a pinch of salt and pepper, and the rosemary and thyme. Cook, without moving the mushrooms, for 2 to 3 minutes to form a golden brown crust, then continue to cook, stirring, for about 3 minutes more, until the mushrooms are well browned and starting to soften. Add the butter and stir to melt it in. Add the stock, shaking the pan very quickly to get the mushrooms to jump and move in a circle; cook for about 3 minutes to thicken the sauce and soften the mushrooms. Remove the thyme, rosemary, and garlic cloves. Taste and season with more salt and pepper, if needed.

OPTIONAL: THE WATERCRESS PUREE:

Combine the watercress, lemon juice, and lemon zest in a blender and blend until smooth. Place in a squeeze bottle. Should you prefer to skip the puree and instead add a few leaves of watercress, like the photo at left, you can, but the puree makes the dish extra special.

FOR THE GRAND FINALE:

Bring the braising liquid from the ribs to a simmer, and warm the sunchoke puree, if needed. Spoon some of the sunchoke puree into the middle of four plates and place the short ribs on top of the puree; drizzle with a little of the braising liquid. Top with the mushrooms and garnish with the watercress puree squeezed from a bottle to paint the plate with a few green dots.

CONTORNI

SAUTÉED MIXED MUSHROOMS
170

ROASTED POTATOES
171

POLENTA
172

GRILLED VEGETABLES WITH PARSLEY-GARLIC PESTO
174

ROASTED BRUSSELS SPROUTS WITH BACON
177

Contorni is the Italian version of a side dish that is vegetable rather than protein based. My mother always told me how important it is to eat your vegetables, but as much as I love my veggies, I think it's important to spice them up a bit to add some excitement to the plate. My grilled vegetables will light up any barbecue party, and the Brussels sprouts anointed with bacon are to die for! In this chapter you will learn how to bring good, healthy food to the plate with plenty of flavor. OK, polenta cooked with cream and cheese may not be the healthiest thing on planet, but it's definitely tasty (and if you go grandmother-style, you can skip the dairy). Polenta is one of the most typical foods from my beautiful region of Friuli, so when you make it, you will start to become a little Friulano. Mushrooms are a passion of mine, and I will teach you the best way to cook them so you can include them in a variety of recipes or serve them solo to dig in to their deliciousness without distraction. Potatoes are a must, and my method for making them, salty and crisp, is a recipe you'll want to have in your vegetable-making repertoire. In Italy we are blessed with some of the most beautiful and tasty vegetables on the planet, and here in New York we benefit from the regional farms that deliver the best of their produce to the greenmarkets throughout the city. Wherever you are, look for farm-fresh to make your recipes really shine!

SAUTÉED MIXED MUSHROOMS

Funghi Misti Saltati

4 tablespoons (60 ml) extra-virgin olive oil

8 garlic cloves, peeled and smashed

1¾ pounds (800 g) mixed mushrooms (such as shiitake, cremini, chanterelle, oyster, and royal trumpet), cleaned (see page 25)

2 sprigs fresh rosemary

2 sprigs fresh thyme

Salt and freshly ground black pepper

3 tablespoons unsalted butter

½ cup (120 ml) beef stock, homemade (page 89) or good-quality store-bought

1 tablespoon chopped fresh parsley

There is nothing better than to walk around the farmers' market at the end of October and browse through all the varieties of mushrooms. It's a sign that fall is here and we are heading into another long and cold winter! When I worked in restaurants in Italy, our menus would be completely invaded by mushroom dishes at that time of year. Mushrooms are so incredibly versatile: You can serve them raw, shaved on a salad, in an omelet, as a side dish for your meat, or you can make a soup with them. I love mushrooms with my pasta (see my Mushroom and Mascarpone Quadratti recipe on page 104) and in risotto, even better when they are mixed with black truffle paste (see my recipe for Mushroom and Black Truffle Risotto on page 86). Remember, there are three rules I follow when cooking with mushrooms: 1) never wash them (unless they are morels), 2) always cook them in a screaming-hot pan, and 3) never overcrowd the pan—otherwise they'll never get crisp.

Serves 4

Heat 2 tablespoons of the olive oil in a large sauté pan over medium-high heat. Add the garlic and cook for 2 minutes. Add half of the mushrooms, 1 rosemary sprig, and 1 thyme sprig and season with salt and pepper (the salt helps to release the moisture from the mushrooms). Sear the mushrooms, without moving them, for 2 to 3 minutes until nicely browned on the underside. Turn the mushrooms, reduce the heat to medium, and sauté for about 5 minutes, until softened and nicely browned all over. Transfer the mushrooms to a baking sheet, keeping as much of the garlic in the pan as you can. Repeat the process for the second batch.

Remove the rosemary, thyme, and garlic and return the mushrooms to the sauté pan. Add the butter and stir until it melts, then add the stock and cook, stirring often, until the stock is absorbed and the mushrooms are completely softened, about 5 minutes. Add the parsley and serve.

ROASTED POTATOES

Patate Arrosto

Who doesn't like roasted potatoes? Crisp, salty, flavorful roasted potatoes ... to me a great steak without roasted potatoes is like a burger without cheese (I had to cook a burger at Chef Gordon Ramsay's BurGR on the Las Vegas episode of *MasterChef*; everyone said that my burger was good, but it was missing the cheese and needed some to bring it up a notch). I love to make these potatoes heavily salted, so go ahead and add as much salt you like!

Serves 4

Preheat the oven to 425°F (220°C).

Line a baking sheet with parchment paper and place the potatoes on the sheet. Add 3 tablespoons of the oil, the paprika, salt, pepper, rosemary, and thyme and mix everything together with your hands to coat the potatoes with the oil and seasonings.

In a large sauté pan, combine the remaining 2 tablespoons of oil with the garlic. Set over medium-high heat and heat until screaming hot. Add the potatoes, flesh-side down, and the herbs from the baking sheet and sear for 5 minutes to brown them. Flip the potatoes and sear them for 5 minutes more to brown them on the other side.

Return the potatoes to the baking sheet and bake for 20 minutes, stirring occasionally. Cut one in the middle to see if it is cooked through, and taste it to make sure it's well seasoned (it's always better to add seasoning when the food is still hot). Return the potatoes to the oven for a few more minutes, if needed, and add salt and pepper, as needed.

2 pounds (910 g) fingerling or small new potatoes, scrubbed and halved

5 tablespoons (75 ml) extra-virgin olive oil

½ teaspoon paprika

1 teaspoon salt, plus more as needed

½ teaspoon freshly ground black pepper, plus more as needed

3 sprigs fresh rosemary

4 sprigs fresh thyme

8 garlic cloves, peeled and smashed

POLENTA

2 cups (480 ml) whole milk

1 cup (240 ml) heavy cream

1 teaspoon salt, plus more as needed

Freshly ground white or black pepper

1 cup (150 g) polenta, either quick-cooking or medium-grain

1 cup (100 g) freshly grated Grana Padano

When I was a young kid, almost every Christmas holiday we would go for lunch at my great-grandmother's house up in the mountains in the Friuli town of Claut. Nonna Catina was my father's grandmother, and she was the classic Friuli grandmother: She would wear a dark-colored gown, long stockings even in the summer, and slippers. Always. She had long gray hair and no teeth. Actually, she had one tooth left until I accidentally hit her chin with the back of my head, and it fell out.

Nonna Catina made polenta in the traditional way. There was no such thing as instant polenta for her. She would make it in a very large copper kettle placed on a stand set into the fireplace, and she would stir it for an hour or so with a long wooden spoon. Polenta is a humble and traditional food from the beautiful cornfield-filled region of Friuli, and Nonna Catina was very proud of her polenta. Her love for polenta was passed down to me, and there is no winter month that passes that I don't make it. I love it with braised meat, sausage, and mushrooms, and also served with cheese. I could write a whole book just about polenta! My mother doesn't really approve that I put milk, cream, and cheese in mine (the traditional style uses just cornmeal and water), but when you try it, you will understand why I do it. I generally use Grana Padano, but you can use any cheese: Fontina, Gorgonzola, or goat cheese are good options. A mix of four different cheeses will make the famous *polenta ai quattro formaggi*. If you use a blue cheese, pair it with three milder cheeses—anything except goat cheese, but goat cheese on its own makes a great goat-cheese polenta.

For this recipe, you can use medium-grain polenta or cornmeal and stir the pot for 45 minutes, or buy instant polenta that will be ready in 3 to 4 minutes. I think the instant is just as good, but don't tell that to an Italian grandmother!

Serves 6

In a large heavy-bottomed saucepan, combine the milk, cream, and 2 cups (480 ml) water and bring to a boil over medium-high heat. Add the salt and season with pepper.

Slowly pour the polenta into the milk mixture, bring back to a simmer, reduce the heat to medium, and stir or whisk without stopping for 4 minutes as the mixture starts to thicken. If you've used quick-cooking polenta, add the cheese and you're done; if you're using medium-grain polenta, then you'll go the Italian grandmother route: Reduce the heat to low and cook for about 45 minutes, stirring often, until the polenta becomes very thick and pulls away from the sides of the pan.

Stir in the cheese. If at any point you feel the polenta is getting too thick, stir in a little more water. Pour the polenta into an oval serving plate and serve immediately.

VARIATIONS:

Grilled Polenta: Brush a baking sheet with softened butter. As soon as the polenta is done, pour it onto the baking sheet in an even layer, smoothing the top with a rubber spatula. Let cool completely, then refrigerate until firm, about 2 hours. Cut the polenta into rectangular slices and grill them on an outdoor grill or a very hot oiled griddle pan or nonstick pan until well browned, almost charred, on both sides.

Italian Grandmother–style Polenta: Omit the milk and cream and make the polenta with 5 cups (1.2 L) of water instead. Grandmother-style polenta can be deep-fried (the polenta cooked with cheese won't work, because it doesn't keep its shape when fried): As soon as the polenta is done, pour it onto the baking sheet in an even layer, smoothing the top with a rubber spatula. Let cool completely, then refrigerate until firm, about 2 hours. Cut the polenta into large French-fry shapes or small potato-tot shapes, deep-fry them (see page 57), sprinkle them with salt, and eat them while they're hot.

GRILLED VEGETABLES WITH PARSLEY-GARLIC PESTO

Verdure Grigliate

4 Italian eggplants (about
1 pound/455 g each), peeled
and cut lengthwise into slices
⅛ inch (3 mm) thick

Salt

2 cups (480 ml) extra-virgin
olive oil, plus more for cooking
the vegetables

2 medium summer squash,
cut lengthwise into slices ⅛ inch
(3 mm) thick

2 medium zucchini, cut
lengthwise into slices ⅛ inch
(3 mm) thick

Freshly ground black pepper

7 ounces (200 g) anchovies
marinated in olive oil (about 1
cup)

6 garlic cloves, peeled and
smashed

2 tablespoons finely grated
lemon zest

½ cup (120 ml) fresh lemon
juice, from about 4 lemons

1 cup (40 g) chopped fresh
parsley

This is a great summer side, inspired by a garlicky meat marinade a friend of my father's made for a barbecue back home in Italy, and it's perfect to serve with grilled meat or fish. You'll need to get it ready ahead of time so the vegetables can marinate overnight and soak up all those delicious juices. The hardest part is slicing the vegetables. If you have a slicer or a mandoline at home, you will be fine; if not, you can ask the person at the deli counter to slice them for you (make sure you give her a tip, and she will remember you the next time!). If a knife is your only option, just be very careful and go slowly so your slices come out even.

Serves 8

Line two baking sheets with a double layer of paper towels and lay the eggplant slices over them. Lightly sprinkle the eggplant with salt. (This process is called degorging; it helps to bring the moisture out of the eggplant so when it's cooked it will get crisp rather than soggy.)

Line a separate baking sheet with parchment paper and set aside (if all your baking sheets are being used for the eggplant, use a platter or a few plates). Drizzle a little oil into a large sauté pan or grill pan and wipe the pan with a paper towel. Set the pan over medium-high heat and heat until screaming hot. Lay down enough squash and zucchini slices to fill the pan and cook for 3 to 4 minutes, until browned and turning translucent. Drizzle some more oil over the vegetables and cook for 3 to 4 minutes more, until browned on the other side. Transfer to the prepared baking sheet. Season the vegetables very lightly with salt and pepper. Continue cooking the squash and zucchini slices in batches in the same fashion until all the slices are cooked. Add more oil to pan with each batch. Note that the pan will get hotter as you continue to cook, and the vegetables may burn if you don't keep a watchful eye; you may need to lower the heat a little and cook for a minute or so less on each side.

Pat the eggplant with paper towels. Cook them in the same pan and in the same manner as you cooked the vegetables, using about twice as much oil in the pan as you did for the squash and zucchini.

In a food processor, combine the 2 cups (480 ml) of oil, the anchovies, garlic, lemon zest, lemon juice, parsley, and 1 teaspoon of pepper. Process for a minute or so. The marinade will not need any salt, because the anchovies are already very salty.

Arrange a layer of the vegetables in a glass casserole dish or baking dish. Cover with some of the marinade and repeat with additional layers of vegetables and marinade until all the vegetables have been used. Cover and refrigerate overnight before serving. Keep the vegetables in the marinade when serving.

LUCA'S TIPS: Using a mandoline can be very dangerous if you don't pay close attention and use a hand guard. If you don't believe me, just ask *MasterChef* contestants Lynn and Jessie (they both cut themselves using a mandoline on the show).

ROASTED BRUSSELS SPROUTS WITH BACON

Cavolini di Bruxelles con Pancetta

I have always had a passion for Brussels sprouts. Salty, crunchy, almost burned, that's how I love them! The best is when they are cooked in bacon fat—plenty of it, so you can really taste the bacon. This bacon-heavy Brussels sprouts dish is one I made for a successful *MasterChef* challenge as a side to my spice-rubbed grilled pork chops. The secret is to render the fat from the bacon very slowly and use that fat to coat and cook the Brussels sprouts to perfection. My wife doesn't like to eat pork, so I've made this dish with turkey bacon. Forget about it! Don't waste your time; it will never taste the same.

Salt

8 ounces (225 g) Brussels sprouts, ends trimmed

½ cup (about 3 ounces/85 g) finely chopped bacon

Freshly ground black pepper

1 tablespoon freshly grated Grana Padano

Serves 4

Preheat the oven to 425°F (220°C). Line a baking sheet with parchment paper. Fill a large bowl with ice and water to make an ice bath.

Bring a medium saucepan of salted water to a boil. Add the Brussels sprouts and cook for about 3 minutes, until softened but still crisp. Drain, then transfer to the ice bath and let cool for a minute. Drain and pat dry with paper towels, then cut the Brussels sprouts in half and set aside.

Heat a medium sauté pan over medium heat. Add the bacon. You are going to cook it very slowly because you will need to render all the fat and crisp it up. This will take about 10 minutes. Using a slotted spoon, remove the cooked bacon from the pan and set aside in a small bowl, leaving the rendered fat in the pan. Set the pan over high heat, and when the bacon fat is very hot, add the Brussels sprouts, cut-side down, and sear for 4 to 5 minutes, until well browned, almost burned, on the underside and almost completely cooked through. Turn the sprouts; return the bacon to the pan and cook all together for a minute. The bacon may be very salty, so you may not need to add any salt, maybe just some black pepper. Anyway, we still need to add the Grana Padano, another salty element, so be careful with the salt!

Transfer the Brussels sprouts and bacon to the prepared baking sheet, sprinkle with the cheese, and bake for about 5 minutes, until the cheese has melted. Transfer to a bowl and serve immediately.

DOLCI

**ZABAGLIONE WITH
MIXED BERRIES**
180

CAPRESE PANNA COTTA
182

TIRAMISÙ
187

CHOCOLATE SALAME
189

NONNA ANITA'S FRITTERS
192

APPLE CAKE
194

I love my desserts, but before *MasterChef* I was never big on making them myself. To get baking right, you need to follow the rules, and it's just not in my personality to stick to a recipe to the letter. I would get very frustrated when I'd follow all the steps, but my cake or pie didn't turn out how I'd expected. Through *MasterChef* I learned that baking is like chemistry; you need to understand the process behind every recipe to get it right. I was lucky enough to be given cooking lessons by my *MasterChef* mentors Gordon Ramsay, Graham Elliot, and Joe Bastianich, the best in the business, and now I can say that I can bake. That said, in this chapter you will not learn how to make the world's best apple pie, and you will not surprise your friends with stunning cupcakes either. I'll leave those to books of the many talented pastry chefs among us. What you will learn here is how to make all of my favorite desserts, simple Italian classics, all easy to make. These desserts mean so much to me: My nonna Anita's zabaglione, fritters, and apple cake bring back memories of growing up in Italy, as does my nonna Nori's chocolate salame, and my mother's tiramisù represents my first steps in the kitchen, from arranging the cookies to licking the bowl at the end. And I'm really excited to teach you how to make the dessert that helped win me the title of MasterChef, my world-famous basil panna cotta!

ZABAGLIONE WITH MIXED BERRIES

Zabaglione con Frutti di Bosco

FOR THE BERRIES

1 cup (150 g) fresh strawberries, hulled

1 cup (150 g) fresh blackberries

1 cup (150 g) fresh raspberries

1 cup (150 g) fresh blueberries

¼ cup (60 ml) white wine

¼ cup (60 ml) fresh lemon juice, from about 2 lemons

2 tablespoons sugar

2 tablespoons finely chopped fresh mint leaves

FOR THE ZABAGLIONE

6 large egg yolks

⅓ cup (65 g) sugar

2 tablespoons Grand Marnier

TO SERVE

Brown sugar (optional)

4 to 6 fresh mint leaves

My nonna Anita's three favorite words to me were, "Are you hungry?" She loved to make me *merendas*, or afternoon snacks, and I'd dip cookies into her zabaglione ("custard") as soon as it came out of the bowl. You can make this as simple or fancy as you like, serving it in plain jelly jars or in martini glasses topped with torched brown sugar as a special party dessert. The alcohol can be varied—marsala, Kahlúa, or Baileys are all good choices to change up the flavor. Start your zabaglione when you are ready to serve, and no sooner. It cannot be made in advance!

Serves 4 to 6

FIRST, WE'LL JUICE UP THE BERRIES:
Combine the strawberries, blackberries, raspberries, and blueberries in a large bowl. Stir in the wine, lemon juice, sugar, and mint. Cover and refrigerate for at least 3 hours or overnight, stirring occasionally.

NOW MAKE THE ZABAGLIONE:
Fill a large saucepan with 4 inches (10 cm) of water and bring to a simmer over medium-low heat.

Place the egg yolks in a heat-proof bowl that will fit into the pan snugly without touching the water (you don't want the bowl to touch the simmering water at any point) and, using a whisk or handheld electric mixer, whisk in the sugar, then the Grand Marnier. Whisk until well-combined and foamy.

Set the bowl over the simmering water. Start to whisk vigorously by hand or turn the mixer to high speed. You cannot leave the egg yolks alone for even two seconds—you have to keep on whisking and whisking and whisking to incorporate air into your zabaglione. Whisk until the mixture starts to come away from the sides of the bowl, is very thick and frothy, has more or less tripled in volume, and falls into ribbons when dropped from the whisk. The total whisking time will be 10 to 15 minutes. Remove the bowl from the pan and give the zabaglione a few turns of the whisk to thicken it a bit more.

TO SERVE:

Divide the berries among four to six clear glass dessert bowls or martini glasses, making sure you get a little but not too much of the juice in each glass. Pour the zabaglione on top of the berries. Sprinkle some brown sugar, if using, on top of the zabaglione and burn it with a crème brûlée torch to make a thin crust. Garnish each glass with a mint leaf and serve immediately.

VARIATION

Sponge Cake and Cookie Zabaglione: Cut some sponge cake into cubes and crush a few cookies into large crumbs; layer the cubes and crumbs with the zabaglione in a dessert glass and top with the berries.

LUCA'S TIP: Be sure to make your zabaglione on the thick side, so when you add the berries, their juices they don't bleed into the custard.

Custard, Not Scrambled Eggs

Continuous whisking is the way to perfect zabaglione. If you leave the whisk at any point while you're cooking your custard, you'll wind up with scrambled eggs. If you cook your eggs too fast over too-high heat, this can also scramble your eggs. You can take a peek at the water every so often to check that it's at a simmer rather than boiling. If it's boiling, reduce the heat and take the bowl away from the water for a few seconds (but keep on whisking while it's off the heat!), and then set the bowl back on the pan. Just keep whisking, and you will soon have a silky-sweet reward.

CAPRESE PANNA COTTA

Panna Cotta alla Caprese

FOR THE PANNA COTTA

1½ teaspoons powdered gelatin

2 cups (480 ml) heavy cream

½ cup (100 g) sugar

1½ teaspoons vanilla extract

Leaves from 2 to 3 bunches
fresh basil

FOR THE JAM

3 large plum tomatoes, cored,
seeded, and finely chopped

1 cup (200 g) sugar, plus more
if needed

¼ cup (60 ml) sherry vinegar

FOR THE CREAM

½ cup (115 g) imported Italian
mascarpone cheese (such as
Galbani or Polenghi), at room
temperature

1 tablespoon honey

TO SERVE

Basil sugar (optional; see page
185)

Small edible flowers, such as
violets, radish blossoms, or blue
borage (optional)

When I presented this dessert to the judges at the *MasterChef* finale,
Chef Gordon Ramsay asked if I was going nuts! This is a take on the classic
appetizer *mozzarella alla caprese* that's made with buffalo mozzarella,
fresh tomatoes, and basil. It's a tribute to classic Italian food, as it features
some of the most traditional ingredients and also resembles the colors of
the Italian flag.

Yes, I turned an appetizer into a dessert.

I used to follow what every recipe tells you to do, to put in a whole
packet of gelatin (which is 2½ teaspoons) to set the *panna cotta*. I did this in
the finale, and the judges told me the flavor was there but that they would
have liked to see it a little more jiggly. So much for following recipes without
question! Now I make my panna cotta with less gelatin, and when you put it
on the plate, it moves like an earthquake!

Serves 4

FIRST, WE'LL GET THE PANNA COTTA GOING:
Lightly oil four 6-ounce (180-ml) ramekins or small bowls. Another
option—my favorite—is to use martini glasses; do not oil.

Pour 2 tablespoons of water into a small bowl. Dust the gelatin lightly on
top of the water and let it stand for 5 to 10 minutes to soften.

Meanwhile, in a medium heavy-bottomed saucepan, combine the cream,
sugar, vanilla, and leaves from 1 bunch of the basil. Set over medium-
high heat and bring just to a boil, stirring to dissolve the sugar. Turn
off the heat and transfer the cream mixture to a blender. Run it for 30
seconds, then add the second batch of basil leaves and run the machine
to break them down, about 15 seconds. (The uncooked basil leaves
keep the color a nice bright green.) Strain the mixture through a fine-
mesh strainer lined with cheesecloth back into the original pan, set it
over medium-high heat, and return to a boil. Turn off the heat, add the
softened gelatin, and stir or whisk for about 30 seconds, until the gelatin
is completely dissolved.

(continued)

Pour the mixture into the prepared serving containers and let cool to room temperature. Refrigerate the cooled panna cotta until set, about 3 hours; then, if you're not serving right away, press plastic wrap directly onto the surface of each panna cotta and keep refrigerated until ready to serve.

MAKE THE TOMATO JAM:

Place the tomatoes in a saucepan and place over high heat. Add the sugar and stir constantly until it is absorbed and there is no liquid remaining in the pan, 10 to 15 minutes. Make sure to keep on stirring; if the tomatoes burn just a little, they will become bitter. Add the vinegar and stir until it is absorbed. Taste; if it's too acidic, add some more sugar. You are looking for a sweet jam; the vinegar is added just to balance the flavors. Remove from the heat and cool.

NEXT, MAKE THE CREAM:

In a medium bowl, very gently mix the mascarpone with the honey until the honey is incorporated. Cover and refrigerate.

TO SERVE:

Run a thin knife around the inside of each container to unmold the panna cotta. Invert them onto individual dessert plates. If you're using martini glasses, serve them straight from the glasses as-is. Top each serving with a dollop of the tomato jam and a few dots of the mascarpone cream (you can put the cream in a squeeze bottle and squeeze it out for restaurant-style presentation, if you like), and sprinkle with some basil sugar, if using, getting as creative as you like with your decorations. If you want to get super-fancy, finish the plate with some edible flowers.

VARIATIONS

Vanilla Panna Cotta: Use the seeds from 1 vanilla bean instead of the basil, and bring the mixture to a boil before adding the gelatin.

Berry Compote Option: Instead of making the tomato jam, combine ½ cup (75 g) fresh blueberries with 3 tablespoons of fresh lemon juice and a pinch of salt in a medium saucepan and cook for 5 minutes over medium heat. Add ¼ cup (50 g) sugar and cook for 5 minutes more. Pour into a medium bowl, add ½ cup (75 g) blackberries and ½ cup (75 g) raspberries, and stir in 1 tablespoon chopped fresh mint leaves. Let cool completely and serve with your basil panna cotta instead of the tomato jam.

Basil Sugar

On the *MasterChef* finale, I topped my caprese panna cotta with basil sugar for that extra-special finish. If you decide to make it for your panna cotta, it will put it over the top!

Leaves from 1 bunch fresh basil

2 cups (400 g) granulated sugar

Line a baking sheet with parchment paper. In a food processor, process the basil leaves until the pieces are as small as you can get them (the basil will turn dark; that's OK). Transfer the basil to the bowl of a stand mixer fitted with the whisk attachment. With the machine running, gradually add the sugar until it is incorporated. The wet basil will attach to the sugar, changing its color. You may need more sugar; it's ready when it feels almost dry to the touch, as if it's just granulated sugar exposed to a little moisture (though not wet).

Lay the basil sugar on the prepared baking sheet and cover it with another sheet of parchment to keep flies away. Set aside to air dry for a couple of hours, then transfer to a jar with a lid. Refrigerate until ready to use. It will keep in the refrigerator for about 3 days; freeze any that you don't think you'll be using in that time. One fun way of using leftover basil sugar is to torch it onto the top of a vanilla crème brûlée.

LUCA'S TIPS: *Panna cotta* means "cooked cream," and it's little more than that, but it can be so much more when you do it right. After you've made it once, you'll see how you can flavor it in so many ways, and the best part about it is that it takes less than ten minutes to set up.

To get a nice color into your basil panna cotta, keep adding fresh basil while blending until it's a beautiful bright green.

When you're making the mascarpone cream, think of mascarpone as a beautiful flower: It is very sensitive and needs to be treated right. If you don't mix it with the honey very gently, it will break. I like to take the mascarpone out of the fridge ahead of time so it is easy to mix the honey into it. And please favor imported Italian brands—I recommend Galbani or Polenghi.

You'll have some tomato jam left over: Try spreading some onto bread and top with a fried egg for an egg and tomato jam sandwich.

TIRAMISÙ

I know, there are hundreds of cookbooks out there with tiramisù recipes. But this is my mother's recipe, and it means a lot to me! The first memories of being in the kitchen with my mom were of making tiramisù, and if I eat a bowlful with my eyes closed, I can dream that I am a kid again. I used to help Mom dip the cookies in the coffee and layer them in the casserole while she was preparing the mascarpone cream, and the best part was when Mom let me lick the bowl at the end.

I do just two layers of cookies for a tiramisù that's on the light side, and I like to use Pavesini or Plasmon cookies (which you'll find in Italian groceries and some supermarkets) rather than the standard Savoiardi, or ladyfingers, as they are firmer and absorb less coffee and get less mushy in the finished tiramisù. If you use ladyfingers, it's best if you eat the tiramisù the same day you make it.

Note that this recipe uses raw eggs. Only use super-fresh organic farm eggs. If you are uncomfortable with raw eggs, use pasteurized eggs.

Serves 8 to 10

Pour the coffee into a small bowl and add the brandy and 2 tablespoons of the granulated sugar; stir to dissolve the sugar. Set aside.

In the bowl of a stand mixer fitted with the whisk attachment, combine the egg yolks with the remaining granulated sugar and the lemon zest and beat on medium-high speed until thick and pale yellow, about 2 minutes. Add the wine, and mix to combine. Gently fold in the cheese with a spatula or a wooden spoon.

In a clean bowl of the stand mixer with a clean whisk attachment (or using an immersion blender with the whisk attachment), whip the egg whites with the cream of tartar on medium-high speed until stiff peaks form. Gently fold the egg whites into the cheese mixture.

One by one, dip the cookies very quickly into the coffee mixture and arrange them in a 9-by-13-inch (23-by-33-cm) glass casserole dish, covering the bottom to make a base. The cookies can overlap a little. Cover with half of the cheese mixture. Make another layer of cookies, dipping them into the coffee as you add them. This time you don't need

(continued)

1 cup (240 ml) freshly brewed coffee, cooled

¼ cup (60 ml) grappa

¾ cup (150 g) granulated sugar

6 large egg yolks

1 teaspoon freshly grated lemon zest

¼ cup (60 ml) marsala wine

1 pound (455 g) imported Italian mascarpone cheese (such as Galbani or Polenghi), at room temperature

4 large egg whites

½ teaspoon cream of tartar

10 ounces (280 g) Pavesini or Plasmon cookies

Dark cocoa powder, for dusting

Confectioners' sugar, for dusting

to overlap them, just place them next to each other. Top with the rest of the cheese mixture, smoothing it evenly with a rubber spatula. Cover with plastic wrap and refrigerate for at least 3 hours, or overnight.

Just before serving, dust the top with cocoa powder and confectioners' sugar.

VARIATION

Kids' Tiramisù: Dip the cookies in apple juice instead of the coffee-brandy mixture. Omit the marsala, and add chopped strawberries or peaches between the layers.

A PUFF PASTRY MIRACLE

Everyone knows I've struggled with dessert, but on MasterChef I really learned to believe in myself! This was the first time I ever used puff pastry and, miraculously, this dessert got me in the top three of that challenge.

CHOCOLATE SALAME

Salame di Cioccolato

Nonna Nori, my father's mother, used to make this for us a lot. She passed away many years ago, but I have great memories of spending summers with her, Nonno Toni, and Nonna Catina up in the house in the mountains.

Now, I know some people might have concerns about including raw egg in your salame. If that's the case for you, you can use pasteurized eggs or do without the eggs altogether. In Italy this wasn't something we thought about, as we always had the freshest of eggs. My nonna Nori used to tell me about how when my dad was a kid, he would go into the henhouse, grab an egg or two while they were still warm, make a hole in them with a needle, drink the yolk, and put the eggs back. Then when my grandmother would go to pick up the eggs, they would be empty!

The dark chocolate gives a fudgy feeling to the salame; to lighten it up you could use all semisweet chocolate or a mixture of semisweet chocolate and milk chocolate and decrease the amount of sugar. A final dusting of confectioners' sugar gives your salame an "authentic" aged look.

Makes 1 large or 2 small salames

Fill a large saucepan with 4 inches (10 cm) of water and bring to a simmer over medium-low heat. Place the chocolate in a heat-proof bowl that will fit into the pan snugly without touching the water (you don't want the bowl to touch the simmering water at any point) and set the bowl over the simmering water. Melt the chocolate, stirring occasionally with a rubber spatula. Remove the bowl from the pan and let cool completely.

We'll make the salame batter quickly so the butter doesn't start to melt before you roll it out. Place the butter in a large bowl. Add the eggs and granulated sugar and mix until the mixture is thick and the sugar is completely incorporated. Add the crushed biscotti, grappa, and melted, cooled chocolate and stir well, making sure everything is evenly incorporated. The mixture will be a little sticky.

(continued)

5 ounces (140 g) unsweetened dark chocolate, chopped

2 ounces (55 g) semisweet chocolate, chopped

10 tablespoons (140 g) unsalted butter, cut into cubes and completely softened

2 large eggs

½ cup (100 g) granulated sugar

6 large almond biscotti (about 6 ounces/170 g), coarsely crushed

2 tablespoons grappa

Confectioners' sugar (optional)

Whipped cream (optional)

PANNA COTTA PANIC

I had just realized that I forgot to strain the panna cotta (recipe on page 182) and had to start over again. My family and friends in the balcony went completely silent; in the end the suspense made my win even more of a thrill.

Now you can decide to roll two small salames (you can call them pepperoni!) or one big one. Cut out a long piece of parchment paper, place it on a work surface, and roll the chocolate mixture onto the middle of the paper into a log of whatever length and thickness you like, then move it to one side of the paper and roll the paper around the log to mold it. Twist the ends of the paper to seal it like a candy. Cover tightly with foil and refrigerate for at least 3 hours or overnight to firm up before serving.

Remove the chocolate roll from the refrigerator a few minutes before serving. Dust it all over with confectioners' sugar, if using. Place the salame on the table on a cutting board with a knife alongside so everyone can slice their own piece. Serve with whipped cream on the side, if using.

LUCA'S TIPS: Serve your salame on toasted baguette slices for a chocolate salame crostini.

NONNA ANITA'S FRITTERS

Le Frittelle della Nonna Anita

FOR THE BATTER

1 cup (145 g) raisins

½ cup (120 ml) marsala wine

3 large eggs

¾ cup (150 g) granulated sugar

¼ cup (60 ml) whole milk

Freshly grated zest of 1 orange

½ cup (120 ml) fresh orange juice

1 teaspoon vanilla extract

¼ teaspoon salt

3½ cups (435 g) all-purpose flour

1 (¼-ounce/7-g) packet active dried yeast

1 quart (960 ml) sunflower or vegetable oil

Confectioners' sugar, for dusting

FOR THE GANACHE (OPTIONAL)

8 ounces (225 g) bittersweet chocolate, chopped

½ cup (120 ml) heavy cream

¼ cup (25 g) confectioners' sugar

Pinch of salt

This is a dessert served often during Carnival in Italy, a fun time for us kids, as we'd get to go to school with masks on our faces. I choked up when I was testing this recipe for the book because the smell in the house reminded me so much of my nonna Anita's kitchen. She passed away recently, before she could help me write down how she made these fritters. Luckily, my mom remembered, and it would have made Nonna Anita happy to know that I am staying true to her recipes. I was in Italy the last week she was alive, and she got to know that I had become a MasterChef and was pleased about all I'd learned from her.

I've added a recipe for pastry cream and chocolate ganache to dip your fritters in, but you could also stay simple and do what Nonna Anita would do: Dip them in red wine before popping them into your mouth.

Makes about 3 dozen fritters

LET'S GET THE BATTER GOING:
In a medium bowl, soak the raisins in the wine for 30 to 60 minutes.

In a large bowl, whisk the eggs and granulated sugar. Add the milk, orange zest, orange juice, vanilla, and salt and whisk until incorporated.

Sift the flour and yeast into a large bowl, and whisk to combine. Gradually add the flour mixture to the egg mixture. Add the soaked raisins and their liquid. Cover with a clean dish towel and set aside for 2 hours, or until doubled in volume.

Meanwhile, prepare the sauces to serve with the *frittelle*, if you are so inclined (and I hope you are!).

MAKE THE CHOCOLATE GANACHE:
Fill a large saucepan with 4 inches (10 cm) of water and bring to a simmer over medium-low heat.

Place the chocolate in a heat-proof bowl that will fit into the pan snugly without touching the water (you don't want the bowl to touch the simmering water at any point).

In a separate small saucepan, combine the cream and confectioners' sugar, set over medium heat, and bring just to a boil. Immediately remove from the heat and pour the cream mixture over the chocolate. Let stand without stirring for 1 minute, then whisk until the chocolate is melted and incorporated. Whisk in the salt. Set the bowl over the simmering water to keep warm until ready to serve.

NOW WE'LL MAKE THE VANILLA PASTRY CREAM:
In a medium bowl, whisk together ½ cup (120 ml) of the milk, the cornstarch, and the egg yolk to make a slurry.

In a small saucepan, combine the remaining ½ cup (120 ml) milk, the sugar, and butter. Scrape the seeds from the vanilla bean, add them to the pan, and set the pan over medium heat. Bring to a boil, then immediately turn off the heat and very slowly (to keep from curdling the egg yolk) pour the mixture into the slurry, whisking continuously. Pour the mixture back into the pan and set over medium heat. Whisk continuously until the mixture comes to a simmer, then continue to whisk for another minute or so, until it has thickened into a pastry cream.

IT'S TIME TO FRY OUR FRITTERS:
Heat the sunflower or vegetable oil in a deep-fryer or a shallow saucepan over medium-high heat until a deep-fry thermometer registers 325°C (165°C). You don't want to get the oil too hot, because even though you need the outside golden brown and crunchy, the inside of the dough needs to be completely cooked as well. Line a baking sheet with paper towels.

Make a test fritter: Take about 1 tablespoon of the dough and drop it into the oil, making sure not to burn yourself. Cook the fritter on one side for a minute or so and then turn it. It will take about 5 minutes, turning it at least 3 times. Remove the fritter from the oil using a slotted spoon and transfer to the prepared baking sheet. Cut it in half to check that the inside is fully cooked so you'll know how much time you'll need for the rest of the fritters.

Now start making batches of fritters, 4 or 5 at a time. As they finish cooking, place them on the prepared baking sheet. When all are done and still hot, toss them in a large bowl with confectioners' sugar to coat. My grandmother would serve them at the table just like that. I give you another option for your dipping pleasure: Put the chocolate ganache and vanilla pastry cream into separate serving bowls, set them in the middle of the table, and let your guests have fun dipping their fritters into them.

LUCA'S TIPS: My favorite way to dress up my fritters is to cut them in the middle like a sandwich, spread some pastry cream in the middle, then coat them in the chocolate ganache and top with extra confectioners' sugar.

You could use more dough, if you like, for large fritters; just add a little more time for frying.

FOR THE PASTRY
CREAM (OPTIONAL)

1 cup (240 ml) whole milk

3 tablespoons cornstarch

1 large egg yolk

½ cup (100 g) granulated sugar

4 teaspoons unsalted butter

½ vanilla bean

APPLE CAKE

Torta di Mele

FOR THE TOPPING

1 teaspoon ground cinnamon

2 tablespoons brown sugar

1 cup (150 g) almonds

2 tablespoons unsalted butter, softened

FOR THE CAKE

3 tablespoons unsalted butter, plus more for brushing

1¾ cups (215 g) all-purpose flour, plus more for the pan

Juice of 1 lemon

6 apples

4 tablespoons (55 g) brown sugar

2 teaspoons ground cinnamon

3 large egg yolks

1 cup (200 g) granulated sugar

Zest of 2 lemons

2 teaspoons vanilla extract

2 tablespoons grappa (optional)

7 tablespoons (100 g) unsalted butter, melted and cooled

2 teaspoons baking powder

¾ teaspoon salt

¾ cup (180 ml) whole milk

2 large egg whites

½ teaspoon cream of tartar

This is another of Nonna Anita's classics. I would know she'd made her apple cake as soon as I walked into her house. We'd enjoy a slice or two, and then she'd send us home with a big piece to eat for breakfast the next day. It's perfect in the morning with a good cup of coffee.

Serves 16

FIRST, LET'S TAKE CARE OF THE TOPPING:
Combine the cinnamon and brown sugar in a medium bowl. Pulse the almonds in a food processor until evenly crushed, then add them to the bowl with the cinnamon-sugar mixture. Add the butter and work the mixture with your hands until evenly incorporated.

NOW TO PREPARE THE CAKE:
Preheat the oven to 325°F (165°C). Brush a 9-by-13-inch (23-by-33-cm) baking dish with butter and dust it with flour. Tap out any excess flour.

Fill a large bowl with cold water and add the lemon juice. Peel the apples, core them, cut them into quarters, and then cut them into slices ⅛ inch (3 mm) thick. Place them in the lemon water to prevent them from turning brown.

Melt 1½ tablespoons of the butter in a large nonstick sauté pan over medium heat. Drain the apples and add half of them to the butter. Add 2 tablespoons of the brown sugar and 1 teaspoon of the cinnamon and cook for about 5 minutes, until the apples have softened slightly but still have a little crunch and the brown sugar has started to caramelize; add a little water if the apples start to stick to the pan. Transfer the apples to a medium bowl, and repeat the process with the remaining butter, apple slices, brown sugar, and cinnamon. Let cool completely.

In the bowl of a stand mixer fitted with the whisk attachment, combine the egg yolks, sugar, lemon zest, vanilla, and grappa, if using, and beat on medium speed until thick and pale yellow, about 2 minutes. Add the melted butter and run the mixer for 2 minutes more.

Sift the flour, baking powder, and salt into a small bowl. Alternating with the milk, incorporate the flour mixture into the egg mixture in 3 additions, ending with the flour.

In a clean bowl of the stand mixer fitted with a clean whisk attachment, beat the egg whites with the cream of tartar on medium-high speed until hard peaks form. Using a spatula, gently fold one-third of the egg whites into the egg-flour mixture, then fold in the rest until fully incorporated. Reserve about one-third of the apple slices for decoration and fold the rest into the batter. Pour the mixture into the prepared baking dish, press the reserved apple slices into the top of the batter, and sprinkle the almond topping on top.

Bake for 40 to 45 minutes, until a wooden skewer inserted in the cake comes out clean. Place on a wire rack and let cool completely, then slice and serve.

THE MOMENT OF TRUTH

Even though I was confident in my abilities, I always had it in my mind that I was probably about to go home. It made every moment of the journey that much more exciting!

AUTHENTIC ITALIAN GLOSSARY

00 FLOUR: The preferred flour for making pasta or pizza dough. The number on the flour package indicates how finely ground it is, ranging from 1 to 0 to the superfine 00.

AMARETTO COOKIES: These are a type of Italian macaroon flavored with bitter almonds. The classic is *Amaretto di Saronno*; Saronno is the name of the city near Milano where they are produced.

ARBORIO RICE: An Italian type of short-grain rice used for risotto, named after the town it comes from. I like to use it for my risotto because it is reasonably priced and you can find it almost anywhere.

BRESAOLA: Air-dried cured beef that is aged for at least three months.

CHESTNUT FLOUR: A very sweet flour made from ground chestnuts that's mostly used in desserts. I like to use it with my pasta and gnocchi and balance its sweetness by mixing it with equal parts all-purpose or 00 flour.

EMMENTAL CHEESE: Yellow, medium-hard cheese typical of Switzerland. It has such a distinguished flavor that even though it's not Italian it has become an important cheese in my culinary repertoire.

FONTINA CHEESE: Medium-soft cheese with a tangy flavor profile. It can be produced anywhere, but the original is 100 percent made in Italy and produced only in the region of Valle D'Aosta.

GORGONZOLA CHEESE: Italian blue cheese made in the town of Gorgonzola with a characteristic pungent smell and flavor. The traditional version is *piccante*, which is on the dry side and aged; sweet Gorgonzola is referred to as *dolce* and has mascarpone added during its production.

GRANA PADANO DOP: See Sidebar.

GRAPPA: Classic Italian after-dinner drink made from the skin, pulp, stems, and seeds leftover from wine production. In our kitchen in Friuli you'd be more likely to find grappa in the cabinet than any other liqueur that's typically used in desserts.

Wines of Friuli

I always say that great food without great wine isn't a complete meal. While you are enjoying the recipes from my book, I would like to suggest three of my favorite wines that are uniquely from my region of Friuli Venezia Giulia—a red, a white, and a dessert wine—so you can have a truly authentic and traditional eating experience:

Tocai Friulano: A very well-balanced white wine with notes of apples and wildflowers and a very smooth finish. Perfect with all my appetizers, the lemon-asparagus risotto, and my branzino.

Refosco dal Peduncolo Rosso: A full-bodied and very flavorful red wine with strong tannins. Perfect with hearty dishes like my frico and mushroom risotto and meaty dishes like my short ribs and rack of lamb.

Picolit: A very flowery sweet wine with a distinguished flavor. The word *picolit* means "small" in Friulano, and it characterizes the vine's unique stalk, which grows just a very small number of grapes and hence small batches of wine, making the wine both a rarity and a delicacy.

Grana Padano DOP

Grana Padano DOP is the king of Italian cheeses, one of the most well-known Italian cheeses in the world. It takes its name from its grainy texture and the valley of Pianura Padana in northern Italy (also called the Po River Valley) where it is produced. Grana Padano is a semi-fat hard cow's milk cheese; it is cooked and ripened slowly for at least nine months and then, only after passing strict quality tests, is fire-branded with the Grana Padano trademark. The DOP (*Denominazione di Origine Protetta*, or Protected Designation of Origin) part of the name is key: Only cheeses produced in the Padana area adhering to the Grana Padano requirements can be called DOP. This assures you that what you are buying is 100 percent made in Italy using superior standards.

When I was tasked to cook with Grana Padano on the show it was almost too good to be true: This Italian, through a crazy stroke of fortune, had last pick on ingredients and was left with . . . Italian cheese! The Frico (page 129) and Pancetta-Wrapped Veal Cutlet (page 150) that I cooked in that challenge were made better by the Grana Padano, and this helped me make it into the finals and ultimately win the *MasterChef* competition. Parmesan is also delicious and can be substituted for my beloved Grana Padano in these recipes if that's what's available to you. Just make sure it says made in Italy. There's no substituting that when it comes to cheese!

MASCARPONE CHEESE: Typical Italian cream cheese often used in desserts. I strongly recommend choosing an imported Italian brand such as Galbani or Polenghi.

MONTASIO CHEESE: The most typical cheese of the Friuli-Venezia Giulia region, it is a cow's milk cheese that can be aged for as few as sixty days or as long as eighteen months.

PANCETTA: Italian word for bacon; always made from the pig's belly.

PROSCIUTTO: Salumi made from the pig's thigh, either *crudo* or *cotto*. *Crudo* is dry-cured (prosciutto di Parma or San Daniele are the typical types; I like to use San Daniele because it's made in Friuli, thirty minutes from where I grew up). *Prosciutto cotto* is the cooked version of prosciutto.

ROBIOLA CHEESE: A very creamy cheese made in the Piedmont region of Italy.

SALUMI: Italian word for cold cuts. When you order *un piatto di salumi*, you will get a selection of cold cuts such as prosciutto, salame, mortadella, bresaola, and pancetta.

SAN MARZANO TOMATOES: Plum tomatoes produced in the region of Campania; simply the best in the world.

SEMOLINA FLOUR: This is made from durum wheat and often used in bread making; I like to use it for rolling out my pasta dough to keep it from sticking.

SOPRESSA: A type of salame that is aged and flavored in any number of ways. My friends at Sorriso Italian Salumeria on 30th Avenue in Astoria, New York, make many different types: My favorites are fennel and orange, red wine, garlic, and the classic spicy *sopressa piccante*.

STRACCHINO CHEESE: A very young, creamy cheese typically produced in the Lombardy region of Italy.

TYPICAL ITALIAN MENUS

Menus Tipico

FAMILY-STYLE DINNER FOR LARGE GROUPS
(serve in large platters)

Assortment of crostini and tramezzini 18–43

Prosciutto-Wrapped Figs with Goat Cheese 53

Fried Mixed Seafood with Marinara Sauce 66

My Mother's Lasagna 122

Frico 129

Pancetta-Wrapped Veal Cutlet with Radicchio, Apples, and
    White-Wine Sauce 150

My Mother's Meatballs 158

Roasted Potatoes 171

Polenta 172

Roasted Brussels Sprouts with Bacon 177

Nonna Anita's Fritters 192

Tiramisù 187

SEAFOOD DINNER

Sweet-and-Sour Sardines 60

Salmon, Robiola, and Grape Risotto 77

Branzino with Heirloom Cherry Tomatoes, Fava Bean and Mint Puree,
    and Asparagus Sauce 140

Zabaglione with Mixed Berries 180

MEAT LOVER'S DINNER

Tomato, Mozzarella, and Spicy Salame Bruschetta 31

Chestnut Pappardelle with Braised Veal 112

New York Strip Steak with Vanilla Sauce 162

Chocolate Salame 189

RESTAURANT-STYLE DINNER

Baked Scallops au Gratin 58

Mushroom and Black Truffle Risotto 86

Braised Beef Short Ribs with Chanterelles and Sunchoke Puree 164

Caprese Panna Cotta 182

ROMANTIC DINNER

Clams and Mussels with Cherry Tomatoes in White Wine Broth 63

Linguine with Langoustines 119

Halibut with White Asparagus Risotto 144

Caprese Panna Cotta 182

ACKNOWLEDGMENTS

Grazie!

First of all, I want to thank God for my incredible life.

To my wife, Cate: You are an angel sent to rescue me. Thank you for changing my life.

Thank you to all of my family: my mother, my dad, and my sister.

And my grandparents, the ones who watch me from heaven, and Nonno Toni, who is still here with us.

To all my friends from Aviano, my friends from "*Il Buco*": You have been part of my life for more than twenty years. No other place in the world will ever be like home, because you are not there with me. Thank you for making me feel so special every time I go back to Italy. You are indeed very special to me. *Grazie ragazzi!*

To my "brother from another mother" and best man, Philippe: Most of the memories of my adult life have you in them. *Grazie di tutto! Sei il migliore!*

To my "cousin" Roberto Manfé: I remember the day we met in NYC. We come from the same area; we have the same last name and same personality. You have always been there for me—thank you!

Thank you to my mother-in-law, Diane, for all the long talks about baking and desserts. Thank you to my father-in-law, Michael, because Cate is the most amazing gift I could have asked for.

And thank you to the rest of my wife's family: Grandma Rosemary, Martha, Mary, TJ, Aubrie, Tommy, Parker, James, Matt, Kristy, Trinity, Michael, Jayce, Joseph, Christopher, and Bob. Thank you all because you make me feel like family.

To Chef Max: You have been a wonderful friend, an inspiration, and a great help in my transformation from home cook to chef. Thank you! Cate and I will never forget the amazing meal you prepared for our guests and us on our wedding day!

To Chef Michael Vernon: Thank you for being my true culinary mentor.

To Chef Gordon Ramsay, Chef Graham Elliot, and Mr. Joe Bastianich: Thank you very much for this incredible lifetime opportunity. Thank you for believing in me and for all the amazing and priceless advice.

To the *MasterChef* executive producers: "Mr. Robin" Ashbrook, Adeline Ramage-Rooney, and Yasmin "Yazz" Shackleton. Words can't describe how thankful I am to all of you. Not only for the opportunity you gave me—twice—to be on the show, but also for the way you have always treated me with kindness. *Grazie mille!*

To Brian Smith: You are my hero! To watch a director of your caliber in action so closely is truly a unique experience. Thank you for making me look so good on TV!

To Anna Moulaison-Moore and and "Big Will" Baker: Thank you for everything. You are such hard workers! It was a pleasure to see you working—I felt like I was in a movie! I always watched you with amazement.

To the behind-the-scenes *MasterChef* culinary team: Chef Sandee Birdsong, Brad, Jaime, and Becca: Thank you for the hard work, dedication, and big help. It's inspirational to watch people who are so passionate about their jobs.

There is one person on the culinary team whom I have to thank separately, and you know who you are: Chef Andy Van Willigan. Nobody knows better than you how important you were in my *MasterChef* victory. I could never have done it without your advice. You changed my techniques, my skills, and the way I look at food. I can never thank you enough.

To Princess Perry and Trask "Tractor," the best casting managers that any show could have. You did an amazing job coordinating all of us. Sometimes it's not easy to deal with heavy-headed people like the *MasterChef* contestants, but you always kept your cool, trying to help and make everyone happy. You are two of my favorite people on the whole planet, and I am very glad we are good friends now that the show is over!

To the wranglers: our "bodyguards," as I used to call you: Thanks a lot, guys! Especially to Mr. JP, for being one of the coolest human beings I've ever met! You are an awesome guy and I wish you only the best, my brother! To Jessica—the Vegas days were some of my favorites of the whole show, and you were part of it. To Jeff: That Korean BBQ dinner was one of the best culinary experiences of my whole life. What an epic night!

And to the most important people: I want to thank all of the *MasterChef* contestants. I learned something from each of you. Sasha, Adriana, Malcom, Kathy, Howard, Bime, Beth, Big John, Lynn, Savannah, Bethy, Eddie, Jordan, James, Krissi, Jessie, and Natasha: We all shared a unique experience, and you are all great people! I wish you the best for the future and I'll wait for all of you to eat at my restaurant! Bri: I remember the day we met at the audition. From the determination we both had in our eyes, we knew we were going to see each other again in Los Angeles. Thank you for the long talks and for helping me through some tough moments during the show. Despite your being a vegetarian, I am glad I can call you one of my best friends!

A special thanks also goes to all the people who worked to make this book possible, especially to my editor, Holly Dolce, project editor, Leda Scheintaub, and designer, Danielle Young, who worked so closely with me and helped me through some hard tasks, and to the very talented Tina Rupp for the beautiful photos.

To my friends at the International Meat Market in Astoria: Thank you, not only for the outstanding products and the hundreds of beef short ribs, but for the incredible and warm customer service.

Thank you to all the people at One Potato Two Potato, Shine America, Shine Group, FOX, Abrams, and Triple 7 PR for always being so helpful and very good to me, especially: Monica Austin, Vivi Zigler, Simon Andreae, Rich Ross, Eden Gaha, Paul Franklin, Rob Hughes, Kevin Ivey, Joe Schlosser, Julie Holland, Edwin Karapetian, Ben Liebmann, Alex Mahon, Elisabeth Murdoch, Franc Roddam, Chris Specht, Kelia Tardiff, Marisa Hammonds, Natalia Cianfaglione, Yvonne Bennett, Kelly Perron, Ivana Zbozinek, Brittany Heald, Jaycee Medina, Melissa Gold, and Armando Solares.

Thanks to all of you from the bottom of my heart! *Grazie!*

INDEX

Page references in italic refer to illustrations